outdoor spaces

TEXT

christene barberich

PHOTOGRAPHY

david matheson

STYLING

michael walters

EXECUTIVE EDITOR

clay ide

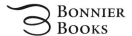

BONNIER
BOOKS

BONNIER BOOKS

This edition published by Bonnier Books,
Appledram Barns, Birdham Road, Chichester,
PO20 7EQ, UK
Website: www.bonnierbooks.co.uk

WELDON OWEN

Chief Executive Officer John Owen
President & Chief Operating Officer Terry Newell
Vice President, International Sales Stuart Laurence

Creative Director Gaye Allen
Vice President, Publisher Roger Shaw
Business Manager Richard Van Oosterhout

Associate Publisher Shawna Mullen
Senior Art Director Emma Boys
Managing Editor Sarah Lynch
Production Director Chris Hemesath
Colour Manager Teri Bell
Photo Coordinator Elizabeth Lazich

Set in Simoncini Garamond™ and Formata™

Colour separations by International Colour Services
Printed in Singapore by Tien Wah Press (Pte.) Ltd.

Copyright © 2005 Weldon Owen Inc. and Pottery Barn

ISBN-13: 978-1-905825-63-9

At Home Outdoors

Our patios, terraces, porches and gardens offer the rare opportunity to extend our living space and to be truly at home in the outdoors. From landscaped grounds to the tiniest city balcony, nearly any exterior area can be the setting for a comfortable outdoor room. The key is to furnish it to reflect the way that you entertain, rest and play. Use this book as your guide to reinvent a patio, garden or porch. With imagination, this space can become much more than a backdrop for the occasional barbeque; it can be as welcoming as the living room and an integral part of everyday life.

We believe that outdoor spaces should be decorated with the same attention to comfort, style and creativity as any other room. Today's new weather-resistant materials and a bevy of stylish, portable furniture options make it easier than ever to create an outdoor space that's truly an extension of the home. Our approach is to provide you with inspiration and accessible design solutions that can be tailored to your own space. In the end, what you will have is an outdoor area that truly reflects who you are and the way you live. And to us, that is the essence of home.

contents

your style

A place that effortlessly bridges inside and out, a green space for gardening, dining, or just getting away, an extension of your living area and an escape from four walls – outdoor rooms play all of these roles and more. An outdoor room is as much a state of mind as it is a proper structure, a setting designed to link the comforts of home with the restorative qualities of nature. Great or small, grand as a poolside pavilion or simple as a city balcony, the best outdoor rooms are easy to maintain and neither too serious nor too formal.

like a narrow terrace or balcony, choose compact chairs and settees you can easily rearrange to accommodate different uses or simply to allow people to circulate freely through the space.

Take a cue from nature itself when choosing furnishings and find fabrics that wear well in the sun and can also take a bit of rain – or a week of it. In a protected space, like a covered porch, take your favourite old sofa outside for the season or set a new one on casters to use in fine weather. To protect your upholstery from sun damage, try dressing furniture for the summer

Indoors, four walls define a room. Outside, a few fruit trees, a flowering pergola, a row of terra-cotta pots, or the curves of a large canvas umbrella set the stage.

Home is where we spend the most time with our families and our friends and no matter what its size or shape, your outdoor space has the potential to become their favourite destination for eating, entertaining, visiting and relaxing. Approach it as you would any other room in the house, with a decorating scheme that celebrates your style and furnishings and accessories that make you feel at home under the open sky.

Think about ease of access, how much storage you need to enjoy your favourite activities and the number of people you expect to fill the space. Furniture placement is especially important when defining a space in the open. For smaller areas,

with weatherproof or canvas loose covers. In a space with little shelter, whether a patio or poolside, invest in tables and chairs made of enamelled metal or weather-tolerant hardwoods, such as teak, redwood or iroko.

When it comes to selecting the style notes that make the space uniquely yours, borrow freely from indoors. A vintage chandelier suspended from tree branches turns an outdoor meal into an occasion, a sisal rug dresses up the floor of a covered porch and a full complement of kitchen accessories transforms a grilling area. It's as easy as that to blend the home comforts of indoors with the delights of being in the open air.

A Family Garden Party

A dappled canopy of leafy trees shelters a family gathering meant to last into the night. There's no need to improve on nature's good taste; just follow it, with a simple table, a light palette and decorative accents that seem to have sprung from the garden on their own.

To guests, a party just seems freer, happier and more memorable out of doors. With imagination and the right amount of planning, it can seem that way to the hosts as well – a collaboration between the landscape and the event that keeps family and friends returning year after year.

Planning an outdoor party for a large group begins with choosing a sheltered site big enough and pretty enough to become a centrepiece in its own right. Select the location based on the best your site offers naturally – a well-kept lawn, a handsome stone terrace, a courtyard paved with bricks or raked gravel. Set your table between a pair of young trees, under a pergola heavy with wisteria or clematis, or in a corner of the garden framed by flower beds and climbing roses. A neatly trimmed hedge or a terrace wall can also help frame a table in an outdoor expanse. In the absence of natural shade, set out wide canvas umbrellas or a canopy for protection and definition. Bring in tall planters filled with staked jasmine or honeysuckle to filter the sun as it lowers in the sky and place a pot of flowers at each of the four corners of your dining area to clearly set it off and keep the space green and leafy. Remember that what gives an outdoor room its charm is a sense of enclosure.

Fresh green accents, *left*, in seat cushions and water glasses echo the vibrant hues of surrounding trees and bridge the gap between a formal indoor look and a more casual outdoor one. **White linens**, *right*, are crisp and practical for an outdoor table, offering a clean slate for bright strokes of colour.

When planning an outdoor party, the time of day is as important to success as the location or menu. Daylight hours are perfect for lingering over a lazy afternoon meal and enjoying the last rays of the sun. Integrate an informal game of boules, badminton or croquet into the day and provide a clever storage solution for the respective racquets, balls and nets close to the court or playing area.

Lawn games encourage a playful mood at large outdoor gatherings and add a quiet appeal of their own to the scene.

Lay down rows of smooth, painted stones on grass or gravel as an all-weather border to define a game's boundary lines. Galvanised metal tubs make handsome storage containers for everything from cold drinks and ice to sun hats and flip-flops. When they empty out at day's end, the tubs come in handy for collecting stray game pieces or bringing tableware indoors.

A framed blackboard, *left*, leaning against a tree makes a handsome impromptu tally board for an afternoon of games. **White stones**, *right*, form the boundaries of a boules court. At game's end, you can invite your guests to pocket one as a souvenir of the day.

A layered lighting plan bathes a nighttime gathering in a flattering, enchanted glow.

Enchanted evenings depend upon the magic of lighting – the intimate glow of votive lights interspersed with flowers on a festive table, fairy lights twinkling in tree branches, a sentinel line of hurricane lamps casting gentle light from the perimeter. Varying the intensity and source of illumination adds depth and drama to your party site, reinforcing a feeling of enclosure around a core of festivity.

Strung between two rows of saplings, white globe lights lend a sparkling café air to a beautifully laid table. Set buckets of roses at either end of the table to add fragrance without interfering with the serving of the meal. White linens and gleaming glassware – Tuscan-style apothecary bottles for olive oil, sleek carafes for wine, green acrylic glasses for water – perfectly capture the special mood of outdoor dining, a blend of formal and casual that's entirely irresistible.

An abundance of yellow roses, arranged in re-used citronella buckets, glow in evening's low light and give a sweet, informal look to the table setting. Floral and checked patterned pillows elevate wooden benches to party status.

Design Details

Colour Palette

White and varying hues of green, from celery to emerald, favourably accent a sunny garden setting. Choose fabrics with small, detailed patterns and layer tints and shades of each hue to add tonal interest to a simple colour scheme. Accents of black punctuate this white-and-green palette and give the garden atmosphere a more sophisticated air. Whether wicker or wrought iron, garden furnishings in deep green or black are classics throughout the parks and formal gardens of Europe.

Materials

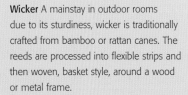

Mulberry trees are hardy and can withstand both city and seaside air, as long as they are sheltered from winds. Fruitless male trees, like those used here, are sought after for creating shade and for growing near paved areas, because there is no fruit to fall and cause stains.

Wicker A mainstay in outdoor rooms due to its sturdiness, wicker is traditionally crafted from bamboo or rattan canes. The reeds are processed into flexible strips and then woven, basket style, around a wood or metal frame.

Pea shingle Typically used in aquariums, pea shingle is a mix of small, smooth stones. The stones come in many muted colours and can be used effectively in various ways in an outdoor space, such as anchoring pillar candles in hurricane lamps or paving walkways.

Big parties call for multiple gathering places for guests to socialise. Lightweight wicker armchairs fitted with removable cushions make ideal seating for a crowd because guests can move them around easily. Arranged in groups of three, they form a cosy conversation circle. Don't forget to place several chairs near the game area, so spectators can cheer in comfort. Make it convenient for guests to set down their drinks by putting out an array of portable brushed metal or plastic tables.

Small groups of wicker or Lloyd Loom chairs, *left*, attended by lightweight galvanised tables, make it easy to move seating around as outdoor activities shift throughout the day. **Glass hurricanes**, *above*, anchored with stones, keep candles glowing when the wind picks up.

playing

Many of us have fond memories of friendly cricket matches at twilight or all-day croquet played in the garden, of afternoon badminton matches that ended in amicable ties or friendly games of tennis that turned fiercely competitive. It's impossible to turn the clock back, but it's easy to make the most of what nature offers us year after year by creating a special space for outdoor games the whole family can enjoy. A designated playing space, a modest investment in some equipment and a place to keep it are all that's needed.

For easy access and convenient cleanup, position storage for games or sporting goods close to your playing area. Enamelled metal cabinets are sturdy, weatherproof and space-saving – but planters, wheelbarrows and canvas holdalls are more fun and look great when filled with mallets, racquets and balls. On a porch or in a sunny garden, set out tables and chairs, then stock an old, weathered armoire with favourite board games, puzzles and playing cards, for a more elegant option. A spacious terrace makes a natural home for pool or ping-pong tournaments; position a weather-

An area zoned for games is an old-fashioned luxury that brings together family, friends and fun. Designate a space for recreation and take the time to play outside.

Make the space for the games you love. Even if you live in town and don't have a large garden, you probably have enough balcony or garden space for a small table and a summer's supply of games and cards. If you're lucky enough to have a lawn, consider setting up your own private boules court or croquet course. Use hedges and flower beds to define the playing field and create a feeling of enclosure. Boxwood is ideal for borders, as is the more fragrant lavender. Both are hardy, simple to grow and easy to care for. Container planters make great moveable boundaries for outdoor games. Shrub roses, geraniums or ivy bring instant life and colour to a playing field.

resistant trunk or a teak console near the game table to hold cues and bats. Whatever you use for storage, make sure it's large enough to keep equipment tangle-free and sturdy or portable enough to protect it from the elements.

Use your imagination to create a playing area that suits your needs. Hang a chalkboard on a nearby tree for keeping score, add a row of chairs and market umbrellas for spectators and set up a beverage station with seating for everyone. If a heated game of tennis is inching toward mealtime, serve dinner courtside with a buffet on a picnic table. All season long, a comfortable play area offers a rare luxury: pure, uncomplicated fun.

A Courtside Retreat

Convert extra space along the sidelines into a lively seating area for cheering players or cooling off between games. All it takes is a few sturdy furnishings and a little stylish storage.

On the tennis court, a versatile seating area set up just beyond the sidelines can be the perfect place for relaxing, conversing and keeping an eye on a close match. Durable furnishings create a convivial setting when arranged in a close formation. For fabrics, think tennis whites: choose bleachable loose covers in canvas or twill and removable white cushions that won't fade during a season of strong sun. A collapsible cabana is a good-looking structure for storing racquets, tennis balls and other gear – plus it's roomy enough to keep extra folding chairs on hand.

Folding shelving units, *left*, offer plenty of storage for courtside essentials. **Bright cabana stripes**, *above*, show up on miniature ceramic planters, adding a sporty touch to the table. **A spacious coffee table**, *right*, is an inviting place to put up your feet between games.

Relaxed Lakeside Living

For those who can't get enough of the water, a ready-made dockside retreat offers the perfect carefree getaway for an afternoon or an entire day. Keep it simple and practical and you can live in harmony with life jackets, oars and waterskis all summer long.

Families with a passion for boating, fishing or swimming are never so at home as when they're by the water. Instead of putting away all the gear and heading straight back to the house after a day on the lake, why not reinvent the boathouse as a multipurpose room? Entertaining and relaxing can mingle with practicality in a waterside retreat for enjoying long afternoons and the last light of day.

Just because an area is designed for storage doesn't mean it can't have the lively spirit of a well-loved room. Make sports equipment a decorative theme: brightly coloured life jackets, striped towels and loops of rope on nautical cleats are necessities that double as striking displays when hung on the walls. Industrial pegboard is designed for storing tools and equipment, but it's also a perfect place to hang a neat grid of holdalls bearing all manner of supplies. Whether as a backing for bookcases or covering a whole wall, pegboard is simple to install. Use it to store everything from sunscreen and extra towels to bathing suits and changes of clothes. This way, when it's time to hit the lake, bringing along all you need is as simple as grabbing a holdall.

A metal café table and bistro chairs, *left*, are lightweight yet durable, making them ideal for a lakeside getaway. A mix of table seating and sectional upholstered pieces is a simple recipe for a flexible space the whole family can enjoy. **A wall of pegboard**, *right* organises holdalls filled with gear.

A boathouse isn't exactly a living room, but it can come close if you choose comfortable furniture that can weather the elements. Striped cotton loose covers are easy to wash and quick to dry and keep furnishings looking fresh. Add a display of framed photographs and memorabilia linked to the outdoor environment to give a sense of permanence to a seasonal room. Make the space equally cosy during evening hours by equipping it with wall sconces for ample light. Water-resistant models designed for the bath are ideal for withstanding humid weather.

A metal boat-rail ledge, *above*, is installed above the sofa as a perch for a changing display of mementos and family photos. **Boating cleats**, *right*, make rustproof hooks for drying towels or hanging waterskiing lines. Attached as handles to a striped piece of acrylic, they make a seaworthy serving tray.

Design Details

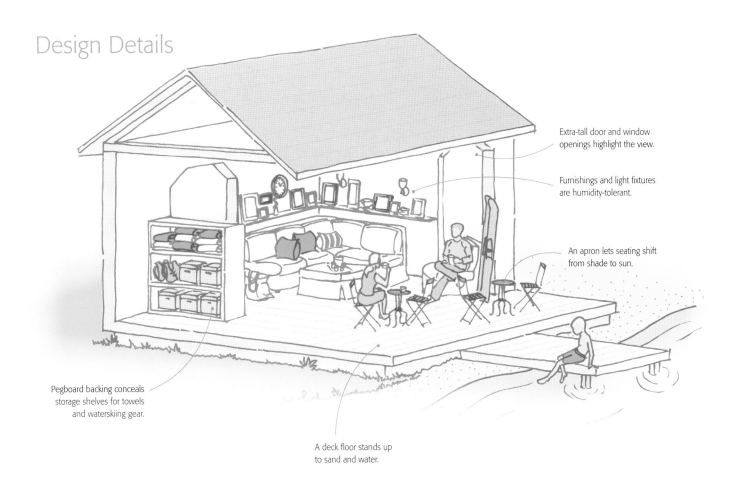

Extra-tall door and window openings highlight the view.

Furnishings and light fixtures are humidity-tolerant.

An apron lets seating shift from shade to sun.

Pegboard backing conceals storage shelves for towels and waterskiing gear.

A deck floor stands up to sand and water.

Colour Palette

Bright reds and blues are traditional nautical hues. For heightened presence, set them against a grey backdrop. This bold palette can make a room look as tailored and trim as a sailing sloop. Soft greys are a savvy choice over white for walls in an outdoor space: grey hides the dirt but, like white, mixes well with many other hues. Red accents are attention-getters outdoors, since blue and green (red's opposites) dominate most landscapes.

Room Plan

Comfortable furnishings, built-in storage and a few clever accessories transform this simple structure with a platform base and plywood walls into an extra room for family entertaining and fun. Walls are sealed with marine paint to cut down on maintenance and to give the interior a polished look. Boat-deck rails become the perfect weatherproof picture ledges that can stay outside all season. A built-in shelving unit is backed with industrial pegboard to provide neat, double-sided storage. Nautical cleats made of rubber are used throughout as wall hooks.

Materials

Pegboard Board perforated with regularly spaced holes into which pegs or hooks can be fitted, pegboard can turn any wall into extra storage space.

Weatherproof fabric The dense weave of canvas or sailcloth can be treated with Teflon (a fluorocarbon) to repel water and resist fading.

Enamelled metal Iron or steel is coated with a thin veneer of enamel, which repels moisture and discourages corrosion.

A Playful Porch

Make the most of a cool breeze by bringing family games out of the house and onto the porch. A table for four, convenient storage and a few strokes of whimsy set the stage for fun and games.

When set up as a playing area, the open layout of a wraparound porch welcomes players and spectators alike. Traditional furnishings, such as a pedestal table, folding director's chairs and a wrought-iron chandelier, gain a fresh look with an entirely black-and-white colour scheme. For a playful atmosphere, decorate with details that reflect the room's activities. String up a deck of playing cards from the chandelier or paint a favourite game board directly on the table. Nearby storage keeps things organised and open baskets leave room for a growing game collection.

Playing cards, *left*, hang from a chandelier as a clever games-room mobile. **A cushioned storage bench**, *above*, keeps family games neatly tucked away. **Quick-fold director's chairs**, *right*, have a lightweight structure that's easy to move around.

How to Store Games and Equipment

As any trainer will tell you, the sporting life's a lot simpler when essential equipment is kept in good order. Organised gear is also a lot better-looking – so good-looking, in fact, that you should show it off while you store it. Let the open framework of a utilitarian rack do double-duty storing and displaying croquet mallets or tennis rackets. Hang bright towels or boating ropes on cleats to give white walls a splash of colour. Label canvas holdalls, so family members can find their gear in a hurry and stock up on inexpensive coolers and tackle boxes for gathering smaller items: their handles make them easy to carry and their shapes make them easy to stack.

Nautical cleats, *opposite*, are normally used to tie up boats, but they also make rustproof hangers for beach towels and waterskiing lines. **A rack designed for croquet mallets**, *left*, can decorate the wall of a potting shed or the inside of a storage cabinet. **Vintage metal numbers**, *top*, salvaged from old signs, find new purpose in an outdoor playing area; just prop them in the sand to keep score for a game of darts, horseshoes, croquet or even tennis. **Miniature clothespegs**, *above*, can be used to secure a few extra badminton shuttlecocks to a light pull or length of string hung from a tree.

cooking

Like open-air dining, outdoor cooking has an appeal all its own. Whether you're cooking at the lake, by the sea or in the comfort of your own garden, the art of preparing a meal outdoors is a skill well worth mastering. Even the simplest menu can feel like a special event when accompanied by vistas of land, sea and sky. And, the pleasure of cooking outdoors is often as satisfying as the meal itself.

Setting up an outdoor kitchen can take as little preparation as wheeling out the charcoal grill, or as much planning as building a fully outfitted can be designed to suit warm weather and three-season cooking. The full range of indoor appliances and cooking gadgets are available in models that withstand the elements, from refrigerators and wine chillers to cookerhobs, gas grills and even wood-fired pizza ovens or roasting spits for gourmet endeavours.

Having all the right tools at the ready is the secret of many cooks' kitchens and it becomes doubly important when provisions are a sprint across the garden. Before heading outdoors, assess and assemble what you'll need. Keep an extra set

From weekend family barbeques to a campfire feast, preparing a meal outdoors has an ease and effortlessness that goes hand in hand with warm weather.

kitchen complete with running water, gas grill and hearth. Whichever approach is right for you, bringing the cooking process outdoors first means finding the perfect location – one with room enough to manoeuvre freely and to contain all the practical elements that accommodate your cooking style. If grilling is your favourite culinary pastime, set up a barbeque station on the patio or decking with a small table close by for tools, platters and seasonings. A fire pit – whether portable or built-in – requires little maintenance and offers a multitude of cooking options, from slow-cooking meats to grilling kebabs. If space is abundant, the outdoor kitchen of your dreams of cooking implements and seasonings in an easy-to-carry container. Forget the one-size-fits-all approach and have some fun: store cutlery in a sturdy wooden box, oven mitts and grilling tools in an enamel bucket or napkins in a glass jar.

Whether you're working at a portable grill or a built-in outdoor kitchen, make sure there's sufficient seating around the cooking area, so that the chef and guests can socialise with ease. An outdoor dining table will serve as the natural focus of the meal at hand, but it always helps to have additional seating near the cooking area for any guests who'd like to be included in the busy preparations or sample the menu.

Casual Beach Cooking

Gathering friends and family at the beach for a cookout is one of the great pleasures of summer. Make it an all-day affair by bringing along plenty of clever, easy-to-transport comforts that invite long hours of lingering well after the sun goes down.

A meal on the beach – whether from an elegant picnic basket, or as the result of a simple barbeque – appeals to outdoor cooks everywhere. The joy of cooking on the sand lies in sharing a family-style meal graced by beautiful weather and the easygoing atmosphere of the water's edge. Stake out a length of sandy shoreline and make classic bonfire cooking a bit more sophisticated with provisions for a portable kitchen. Begin with a food-prep station, an open firepit for grilling fresh fish or vegetables straight from the garden and a seating area where you can happily savour the meal.

Bring along refined kitchen and dining elements that raise the comfort level, yet are still well suited to the beachfront location. Use picnic mats and side tables to help keep sand at bay. Instead of paper plates, carry a stack of your favourite dishes on trays, which can also be used to serve the freshly grilled meal to guests. A three-tiered caddy is convenient for carrying and dispensing glasses. Roll up utensils in napkins, then bind them with string to make them easy to hand out at mealtime. Complete the spread by transferring your favourite fine wines into empty jugs with rock labels.

Fold-up side tables, *left*, are useful for their quick-to-set-up design and lightweight portability. A bounty of baskets and trays makes easy work of toting dinnerware. **Smooth stones**, *right*, are labelled with chalk to identify wines while paying tribute to the charm of a beachfront destination.

Sitting on the sand all day, even when it's soft, leaves much to be desired in the way of comfort. Borrow cushions from your sofa and use boulders as a natural framework for an outdoor lounging area. Select washable fabrics, like denim and twill, that are durable enough to withstand a full day of dining, sun and fun by the water. Unfurl a length of painter's canvas or a clean dust sheet over the sand to further define the area.
At the beach, cooling tones of blue and sandy shades of beige are a natural colour scheme that you can extend to furnishings, pillows, throws and tableware.

Streamlined folding chairs, *left*, are made with weatherproof fabric. **Tablecloth weights**, *above*, fashioned from beach stones, safeguard linens from offshore breezes. **Denim cushions**, *right,* are piled against an outcropping of rocks to create a natural beachfront "sofa."

Colour Palette

Blue and white have long been a classic colour pairing for seaside cottages and retreats. The addition of sandy beige makes this an easy indoor palette to live with all year-round and in outdoor spaces, it looks as natural as sand and sea. Denim blue is the perfect colour (and material) accompaniment and over time it fades beautifully in fabrics. For a fine finishing touch, add some white accessories in the form of pillows, blankets and table linens, which make the palette more trim and tailored.

Materials

Denim This heavy, twill-woven cotton fabric is very popular. It is an ideal material for outdoor furnishings, due to its durability and washability.

Seagrass A commercially grown aquatic grass, seagrass produces a strong fibre that is similar to straw and smoother than coir or jute. Woven seagrass mats prove resilient even when exposed to high humidity and moisture.

Canvas A heavy-duty fabric commonly used in the manufacture of sporting goods, tents and outdoor furnishings, canvas can be woven from linen, hemp or cotton. Water- and weather-resistant, canvas perfectly suits the casual, relaxed look of an outdoor setting.

The natural fibres of seagrass mats and wicker baskets help define cooking and dining areas, and are perfect for outdoor use because of their durability. As afternoon stretches to evening, provide guests with everyday luxuries to ease the transition to twilight. Keep warm wraps nearby for taking in the sunset. Hang lanterns on stakes to light seating areas, or nestle them in the sand. After dark, hand them out to guests to light their path back from the beach.

Seagrass mats, *left*, are known for their weatherability and for the way they easily shake out and roll up when it's time to head home. **An oversize basket**, *above*, is packed with sweaters and throws, a welcome comfort when cool coastal breezes blow in.

How to Set Up an Outdoor Kitchen

One of the delights of outdoor cooking is improvising solutions from whatever is nearest at hand, whether at the shore or on the dock of a fishing cabin. Try beach rocks to build a campfire for grilling fish, driftwood to frame a fanciful "dining room" on the dunes, or a couple of scrubbed shells to serve up the olives. For dedicated outdoor cooks, a few permanent fixtures make sense: choose materials that stand up to sun and moisture, like stone, teak or stainless steel. Hang a wrought-iron pot rack from a tree limb, or position a simple ladder to provide handy storage for pots, dish towels, condiments and utensils.

A teak storage ladder, *left*, designed for hanging towels in the bathroom has been converted into an outdoor pot rack with a shelf for condiments, herbs and grilling tools. A circle of stones, *top*, is just the right size to hold a grilling tray, borrowed from the barbeque, over the heat of a campfire. Overturned colanders, *above*, are perfectly shaped to keep insects away from food; they can be flipped over to rinse berries for dessert, too. A console table, *right*, carried out to a grill-side location, is easily transformed into a buffet station, with everything at the ready for diners. Look for a suitably shaped plastic cover to keep furnishings protected at night or in bad weather.

dining

Setting the table for a meal outside is always rich with creative possibilities. When fresh air combines with the gentle sway of trees overhead, the feeling of grass underfoot or the sound of waves crashing on the beach, the surroundings demand a table that's equally inspiring. Whether it's a picnic for two beside a river, a simple lunch on the patio or a barbeque for friends, the right table setting adds unique character to the occasion: choose goods that make cleaning up easy afterwards or that show your best china, crystal and linen to new advantage.

Stretch the boundaries between indoors and out and take advantage of the freedom that fine weather affords. Give the wheelbarrow a good scrub and pack it full of candles, dinnerware, cutlery and wineglasses to wheel outside and cut down on return trips to the kitchen. Pull out all the stops and suspend a chandelier from a tree to light a festive table beneath. Or hang a canopy of lanterns and dine by starlight.

When setting up an outdoor dining space, it's natural to consider the season or the weather, too. Warm summer days beckon all things light

Serving a meal under the open sky draws renewed attention to the surroundings and inspires a heightened appreciation for ingredients at their freshest.

Next, let the vitality of the outdoor location take the lead and make the preparations as much fun as the event itself. Honour the occasion with tasteful details and finishing touches. Try creating a special set of picnicware from mismatched flea market finds: line colanders or baskets with napkins and use them as alternatives to plates and bowls. In lieu of linens, cover your table with paper that can be playfully decorated for a meal. Customise picnic benches with individual cushions and create place cards made from shells, smooth stones and other natural objects found in the surrounding landscape.

and tasty and baskets become indispensable serving dishes for such garden fare as fresh tomatoes or just-picked ripe strawberries. Cooler days call for richer dishes served hot, so crockery and warm blankets become part of the set-up.

Think of how much sweeter ice cream tastes in the hot sun, how a burger off the grill always beats one cooked inside and how a sun-ripened strawberry at home is never as juicy as the ones eaten right in the patch. Let these memories draw you outdoors the next time you're planning a meal and you'll instantly be inspired by the delights of dining alfresco.

A Backyard Barbeque

Grilling outdoors is the very essence of warm-weather entertaining.
Enhance this summertime tradition with details that make it special.
For a fresh take on the garden barbeque, reinvent place settings
with amusing touches designed to please hosts and guests alike.

A summer barbeque – even if it's just classic burgers – can be as stylish as it is fun and it needn't take hours to prepare. Take a tapas approach when planning a barbeque menu by offering lots of bite-size options to satisfy both grown-ups and children. In place of the usual-size burgers, try scaling down the burgers and serving two to a plate. With a serve-yourself station of condiments and toppings, guests can customise each burger differently. Adults will appreciate the buffet-friendly portions and kids will find these redesigned favourites more fun to eat. Wrap the mini burgers in greaseproof paper – a nod to no-frills bistro fare – and use the same paper to line miniature colanders. Fill each colander with French fries straight from the kitchen and tuck mini shakers of seasoned salt into each bowl.

The principle of "less is more" works for table settings as well. A mix of friendly hues strikes a festive note and the unfussy style suits the occasion. Simple, sturdy diner-style dishes, cutlery and glassware are practical and just right for the outdoors – a marriage of sensibilities that defines the mood of this backyard barbeque from start to finish.

A terra-cotta planter, *left*, doubles as a convenient holder for keeping the cook well supplied with grilling tools. **Polka-dot cloth napkins**, *right*, become place mats that add a touch of fun to the simplest garden feast – and they're more colourful and child-friendly than plain white.

Create a welcoming mood for your guests by providing several places to relax or visit. Multiple food stations can keep everything guests need within easy reach, which leaves more time for you to enjoy the party. Stock enamelled buckets with soft drinks and wine, making sure you have an extra tub of ice ready as the day warms up. Use extra benches as easy-to-manoeuvre stands for side dishes. And be sure to have several patio umbrellas on hand to shade tables and seating areas and to move around with the course of the sun during a long afternoon.

Enamelled metal buckets, *left*, offer an easy way to keep beverages icy-cold; positioned at the end of the table, they're always ready to serve. The flexibility of picnic benches perfectly suits barbeque-style meals, where mingling is as popular as sitting down to eat. **A porcelain jug**, *above*, hosts a casual bouquet of flowers freshly picked from the garden.

Design Details

Colour Palette

Inspired by the cheerful hues of a wildflower centrepiece, a palette of pink and white, accented with indigo blue (and colourful polka-dot napkins), dresses this outdoor space. Bright tones have a playful energy that reflects the spirit of a garden barbeque and summer celebrations of all kinds. Outside, it is easy to use multiple, bright colours in a carefree mix. In fact, vivid palettes and patterns shine -- while muted colours get lost -- in the brilliant sunlight and open space of a poolside patio.

Materials

Teak Indigenous to the warm, humid climate of Southeast Asia, teak is a notably water-resistant wood and a practical choice for outdoor furnishings. Its rich lustre improves with age and weathering, so teak adds a polished, permanent look to other furnishings in outdoor spaces.

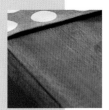

Flagstone An ideal material for garden patios and poolsides, because of both its beauty and durability, flagstone is a hard, evenly stratified stone that cleaves into flat pieces that are well suited to paving.

Enamelware Metal dishware coated in layers of enamel has a retro look that's reminiscent of 1950s diners. Enamelware is also rustproof and has a long-lasting durability, making it suitable for meals in the outdoors or in humid climates.

Relaxing in warm weather comes naturally, but you can make it especially easy for guests by providing furniture chosen for its comfort and versatility. Extra-wide chaises add a luxurious note to garden sunbathing; they also make a cosy platform for a two-person game of cards. Dressed with soft pillows and colourful throws, the hardiest weatherproof seating feels as comfy as the most broken-in sofa. Add pots of flowers to soften a pool's hard edges and all that's left to order up is a day of sunshine and cool breezes.

Double-width lounge chairs, *left*, dressed with towels and plump pillows, invite friends to lounge together. **Flowering plants in terra-cotta pots**, *above*, bring touches of warmth to the cool edges of a pool area or deck. Arranged in rows or clusters, they give subtle definition to the poolside, making selected areas more intimate.

A Tropical Courtyard

By design, a courtyard is a cool place to escape the heat in warm weather. It's also a perfect spot to set up a dining area for a sun-dappled luncheon or a casual dinner with friends. Tropical plants, classic furnishings and accessories in vibrant hues make the most of an open-air layout.

Within the privacy and shelter of four walls, a courtyard falls somewhere between indoors and out, making it equally suited to interior furnishings as it is to sturdier outdoor pieces. Situated between interior rooms, it functions as a lively, transitional space to easily connect indoor and outdoor areas. A courtyard might also serve as the main entrance to a home, as it does here, welcoming guests into an enclosed area shaded by tall tropical plants.

An oasis between the main door and the street, a courtyard is a tried-and-tested place for keeping cool on hot days. Take full advantage of this outdoor room by furnishing it as you would its indoor counterparts – as an elegant dining area with a round table and loose-covered chairs, as a casual living room with an upholstered sofa and a pair of wing chairs, or as a cosy breakfast nook with a table for two. Use unexpected accents, such as the grosgrain belts around each chair here, to add character to the space. The refreshing properties of blue, green and aqua, from the table settings to the sea glass lanterns, keep this spot cool. Plenty of plants and shade trees provide a lush respite from the heat.

Tailored chairs and a limestone table, *left*, have weatherproof plastic loose-covers (stowed in a nearby urn) to protect against passing rain showers. **Miniature succulents in glass votives**, *right*, are placed at each table setting to harmonise with the surrounding landscape design.

A few large pieces installed in an outdoor space form a year-round foundation, making it easy to add accessories to suit the season or a special occasion. Changing the loose-covers on the chairs, or bringing in a completely new seating style, is a simple way to freshen the look or quickly update a courtyard dining area. Furniture of a grander scale, like this limestone table, often works best in exterior settings, where it doesn't have to compete with other furnishings and where ample size stands in proportion to trees and sky. A substantial Turkish oil jar is right at home here, too, amid towering plants and walls framed by bougainvillea.

A large woven tray, *above*, is a helpful carryall for stacks of tabletop items. Set atop an oversize urn, it becomes a makeshift sideboard during lunch.
A pale grey linen tablecloth and muted paisley napkins, *right*, tie together the cooling, sea-glass hues of the glassware on the table.

Colour Palette

If you love the vibrancy and seductive colours of the Mediterranean, use a sea-inspired palette of aquamarine and green to give a courtyard -- or any room -- an energetic island atmosphere. Reflect hues from the terrain of this sun-bleached region, too, by adding touches of pale grey and white in the background. This courtyard does just that, offering a neutral canvas that draws the eye to colourful details, such as the glass lanterns and blue-green accents that sparkle like sunlit water.

Materials

Bougainvillea Also known as "paper flower," this woody flowering vine grows best in warm climates and full sun. With varieties in a range of red, pink, orange, yellow and white, bougainvillea can also be potted indoors in colder climates and brought outdoors in the summertime.

Banana plant From the Musacea family of plants, the banana plant is actually a perennial herb rather than a tree. It thrives in warm, tropical climates and its leaves can be damaged by strong winds, making it ideally suited for sheltered courtyard.

Succulents Perfect for potting because they require relatively little soil to survive, succulents allow you to plant several varieties in the same container. From the same family as cacti, succulents have thick, fleshy stems and leaves that make them extremely drought-resistant and hardy.

Like fabrics and accents used indoors, plants can serve as decorative accessories, softening the look of an outdoor space. A mix of potted and planted landscaping makes it easy to "redecorate" whenever the mood strikes. In this courtyard, a vibrant curtain of bougainvillea has the same visual impact that a favourite painting might have above a fireplace. Arrange plants from short to tall for added depth and texture. A collection of potted plants can easily fill in empty spaces along pathways and in corners.

A shaded dining area, *left*, is perfectly framed by an archway of bougainvillea vines and a canopy of banana leaves. **A silver ice bucket**, *above*, sits in a nearby fountain, a clever, out-of-the-way solution for keeping white wine cool on a hot day.

A Dockside Breakfast

Let autumn's crisp, cool air inspire a weekend breakfast that's both rustic and comfortable. Set up a lakeside cabin for a casual morning meal with camp-inspired conveniences and cheerful colours.

Enjoy a quiet moment with coffee and the newspaper, or serve up a hearty breakfast for friends in an outdoor space that offers all the pleasures of a cabin escape. With the convenience of camp style and the comfort of warm blankets, you can savour a cosy morning meal in a rustic retreat. Bring the setup for a make-your-own breakfast right to the window. Here, a vintage "Home Cooking" sign is hung by a hinge outside the kitchen window to create a convenient shelf and an instant extension to the outdoors. When not in use, the sign hangs as an invitation for future get-togethers.

Accents of bright red, *left and right*, hold their own against softly weathered wood. **A serve-yourself buffet**, *above*, is set up on a windowsill that allows easy access to the kitchen. A vintage sign acts as a shelf.

How to Dress an Outdoor Table

Dining alfresco means eating in the fresh air, which is not at all the same as "roughing it". For an experience at the table that's as fresh as the outdoors itself, forget about folding chairs, paper napkins or plastic utensils and style a tabletop with the elegance and comfort of its indoor counterpart. Focus on portability, using containers and trays that are easy to pack. Choose colours and textures that match the vibrancy of the landscape. Mix "country" with "country club" as the sun strikes a fine cut-glass jug at one end of the table and vintage Speckleware at the other. Remember that it's summer, so bend the rules and have some fun.

A Speckleware table setting, *above*, or Graniteware, as it's sometimes called, lends a casual and rustic note to any meal. On a breakfast table, combine individual coffee jugs with tea-towel napkins, modern juice glasses and enamelled metal dinnerware for a setting that's as cheerful as it is practical.

Establish a theme with tea towels, *right*, used to decorate an ice bucket or stand in as place mats. A lobster dinner can be a messy affair, so you might also use these brightly decorated towels as napkins or bibs.

Enamel bowls, *left*, used as sandwich baskets, are large enough to hold an entire picnic lunch: turkey baguettes, cans of drink and fruit for dessert. A linen napkin tied securely around the fixings gives each basket a pretty handle.

A layered Caesar salad, *below*, is presented on a square tray; dressing sits at the bottom of a bowl topped with leaves of romaine, making a first course that's simple to serve and easy to eat. Creative menus for outdoor dining can be portable without being standard picnic fare.

resting

Few things feel as soothing and indulgent as a peaceful nap, especially when you're suspended in a hammock under the shade of a spreading tree. There's also the lull of breaking waves as you drift off to sleep at the beach or the thrill of catching a glimpse of a shooting star as you snuggle into your sleeping bag. With these restorative temptations in mind, why not scout for a peaceful place in which you can set up an outdoor reading or napping spot?

Begin by looking around for a location that feels removed from the cares of the world: a

Selecting the perfect fresh-air "bed" is the next step. Relax on an oversize blanket, a folding army cot or a fully made daybed. An air mattress or a hide-a-bed stored away for guests is easy to roll outside, but it's even simpler to borrow the cushions from a loose-covered sofa and lay them on the lawn for an afternoon nap. Choose outdoor bedding with the same care you would for any other sheltered outdoor space. Look for upholstery made of sturdy, sunproof fabrics and soft, removable covers that can withstand some dirt and go straight in the washing machine.

A quiet hour in a hammock or stretched out on the soft grass beneath a shady tree can sometimes feel as restorative as an afternoon stay at a spa.

shaded glen at the far end of the garden, a secluded corner, a honeysuckle-draped porch or a patio or balcony enclosed with pots of tall bamboo. Next, you'll want a little shelter for your sleeping space, away from the many distractions of the outdoors. Trees make wonderful buffers to road noises and they provide refuge from midday sun. If woodlands are in short supply, opt for less permanent solutions. A market umbrella will provide shade equally well and adds definition to a treeless space. Sheer curtains, secured to branches or a clothesline, are another way to create shade and a delicate scrim of privacy between you and the rest of the world.

To give your hideaway the distinct feel of a room, add an amenity or two. Set up a portable stereo on a side table for soothing music. Hang a bundle of dried lavender nearby for a relaxing dose of aromatherapy – or suspend an alarm clock to dispel any worries of oversleeping. Set up a tent of mosquito netting to keep out pests and to create a serene feeling of enclosure. Hang a cluster of flashlights or a lantern to read by or add a rug underfoot. Whatever furnishings and comforts you choose, keep your outdoor retreat minimal so you can enjoy the view. After all, getting back to nature is the whole point of this resting place.

A Porch for Napping

When warmer weather arrives, a back porch or verandah can undergo transformation from barely noticed pass-through to inviting outdoor sitting room. Make it a place where a lazy afternoon nap is impossible to resist and where friends will linger on a balmy evening.

Porches tend to be furnished with front-room castoffs – a bit frayed around the edges, short on comfort, dated in style. But they deserve better. A porch is often the best room a house has to offer. Open to sun yet protected from rain, a porch is a delightful hybrid built for enjoyment – a room with not just a view but with a wraparound vista, with not just a window but with open-air ventilation. Because a porch offers overhead protection and an enclosed perimeter, it's the perfect place to set up a relaxing zone filled with summertime reads or a lounging nook fitted with comfortable couches or both.

While a porch swing will always be classic, a white rope hammock is also easy to hang from the beams for a cool summer seat. Customised with a soft headrest tied to the hammock's support bar, this timeless design is hard to improve upon as a place to rest or to while away the day with a friend. Substitute a hanging basket for a side table, putting newspapers, books or bottled drinks within reach. Like shoes and formal manners, lights on a porch aren't mandatory. But a clip-on reading light attached to the railing is a welcome addition for reading past sunset.

A hanging basket, *left*, secured to the ceiling with rope, makes a porch-style alternative to the standard side table when stocked with magazines and refreshments. **All-weather cushions**, *right*, including an attached neck roll, add a layer of comfort to the classic woven-rope hammock.

A corner sofa tucked into the porch creates a welcoming spot to read, write letters or put your feet up with a friend. Made of treated seagrass, this seating is designed for both indoor and outdoor use. Floor and ceiling are painted in a pale shade of blue that has long been used to keep away moths and other insects on the porch. A sisal area rug adds definition to this lounge area and picks up the amber tones of the seagrass sofa. A small side table made from a glass display offers a place to keep and show postcards and other tokens of summer holidays and it holds magazines on a shelf beneath.

A glass display box, *above*, is set atop a table of similar proportions to store favourite postcards, watercolours in progress and photographs. **An enamel pendant lamp**, *right*, remains protected in this partially enclosed area and keeps the porch illuminated long after sunset.

Colour Palette

A palette of ivory, pale blue and navy blue gives the porch of a beachhouse a cooling atmosphere all summer long. Painted in light blue, the floor stands out against ivory walls and has a calming effect that makes the whole space feel restful. Co-ordinating flowerpots, nautical stripes on pillows and navy blue accessories introduce crisp variations on the colour theme. Use clear, true blues like these anywhere you want to beat the heat and create a breezy sense of sea and sky.

Materials

Petunias Hardy and easy to grow, petunias flower all summer long. A single plant will produce hundreds of blooms and its full foliage makes it a natural as a container plant. Use petunias to create a low privacy screen around the perimeter of a porch.

Seagrass A commercially grown aquatic grass, seagrass produces a durable fibre that is similar to straw and smoother than coir or jute. It is most commonly woven into textured, moisture-resistant rugs that hold up well in high-traffic areas, such as porches, hallways and entrances.

Deck stain This stain- and moisture-resistant woodstain may be oil- or water-based, glossy or flat. It is designed to withstand heavy foot traffic and prolonged exposure to outdoor elements.

When displayed inside, flowers picked from the garden help blur the distinction between indoors and out. Here, dozens of easy-care petunias – the same plants used in the surrounding landscaping – are arranged along the porch's perimeter to make the transition even smoother. Painted in various shades of blue that complement the porch's simple colour scheme, the flowerpots also give the space a touch of front-room formality. Known for its calming quality, blue is an ideal choice for any resting space.

Potted petunias, *left*, create a fluttering border of white, pink and lavender along the porch railing. **A vintage-style birdcage**, *above*, makes a witty, portable home for a trio of votive candles.

Daybed in the Shade

ROOM TOUR

On a warm summer afternoon, who doesn't long for a quiet, shady spot reserved expressly for leisurely pursuits? Borrow an idea from the classic sleeping porch and furnish an outdoor space with all the comforts of a guest room and the old-fashioned appeal of a garden gazebo.

For many of us, summertime brings more than just warm weather and time off for holidays; it also means planning for visiting guests. With any kind of overhead structure to offer shade on a sunny day, a porch becomes the quintessential outdoor sanctuary and a perfect spot for reading, resting or simply thinking. Expand on the notion of the classic sleeping porch by furnishing a warm-weather room to create an enticing hideaway for family and visitors.

Bring out some indoor luxuries that can survive a little weather, like a large mirror and a few flea market paintings. For furnishings, select pieces that are versatile enough to make the transition from inside to out. A bath cabinet is suited to porch use because it resists damage from humidity. Likewise, laminated stacking chairs are moisture-resistant and easy to stow away during rainy spells. For comfortable outdoor seating that moves easily to shelter, try fitting a daybed with casters. First made popular by the French in the seventeenth century, daybeds have generous proportions that offer flexibility for both seating and resting. A daybed arranged in the centre of the room is equally inviting for lounging with weekend guests or curling up for a quiet read.

Fragrant wisteria blossoms, *left*, bring luxurious scent and welcome shade to an outdoor room. **An upholstered daybed**, *right*, sits in the centre of the space, inviting guests to relax. With casters attached to each leg, it can easily be wheeled inside during inclement weather.

Design Details

Colour Palette

Take inspiration straight from nature and decorate an outdoor space with pure white, bright leaf green and the light blue of a summer sky. White is never simply white; it changes colour as the day progresses, from rosy in the morning to tints of blue and grey as the light begins to fade. Here, white stands in contrast with the greenery of the garden and emphasises the varied textures of linens on the daybed. Against the white-painted floor, white loose-covered furniture seems to float.

Materials

Cotton This lightweight fabric is woven from spun fibres from the boll of a cotton plant. From loosecovers to linens, breathable, washable cotton is an ideal all-season fabric. Long-staple or Egyptian cottons are the softest options for bedding.

Wisteria The perfect canopy for a sleeping porch, wisteria screens sunlight by day and lets the stars peek through at night. This woody-stemmed climber is dripping with fragrant flowers in early summer and thrives when planted in full sun.

Boxwood This bushy evergreen shrub with its masses of dark green, oval leaves, is excellent for creating enclosure in an outdoor space. The traditional shrub used for mazes in formal gardens, boxwood takes well to topiary and is handsome when used as a pathway edging.

Choosing an all-white palette has many advantages for a porch setting. Any monochromatic colour scheme creates an uncomplicated backdrop, but pure white adds a cooling touch and makes a space feel instantly airy and larger than its actual dimensions. Plus, it's practical: white fabrics won't fade and white finishes are easy to wash or bleach. To add interest to an all-white daybed, layer it with soft textures. Take your cue from the garden and sky by adding small accents of colour in artwork, pillows and throws.

Layered bed linens, *left*, offer an intriguing mix of quilted and smooth textures, unified by a white palette. **Laminated chairs and a glass-front bath cabinet**, *above*, transform a covered porch into a convenient spot for unwinding and talking on the phone.

How to Make an Outdoor Resting Spot

Relaxing on the grass or dozing by the water need not be a pleasure remembered from childhood, when resting was a bonafide pastime. Slow the pace and scout out your own private spot for laziness in the privacy of the garden. Steal quilts, throws and pillows from the bedroom and camp out with books and magazines for the afternoon. Make the settee your outdoor headquarters for a day of reading the paper and sneaking in a nap. Thwart uneven terrain and insect life by unfolding a camp-style cot, then add a little luxury (and shade) with a curtain panel secured to a branch or clothesline. Find a quiet perch in the garden and rediscover the radio or just enjoy the view with a friend.

Sheer organdy, *top*, makes a pretty scrim for a summer courtyard. During the day, it adds privacy and creates shade. At nighttime, it shimmers, with lanterns or fairy lights behind. **A water-smoothed stone**, *above*, keeps a curtain in place and strikes a balance between the rustic and the domestic. **A folding camp stool**, *right*, makes a portable magazine table for a shady reading spot. **A loose-covered bench**, *opposite*, transferred to a sunny corner of the garden, creates a sitting area that encourages visitors to stay all day.

entertaining

Hosting a party under the stars holds the promise of magical memories. From a Sunday brunch to dinner for twenty, one of the greatest advantages of entertaining outdoors is that it opens up the event to generous amounts of space. Open-air locations offer more room for guests to move about and socialise – provided the weather cooperates. And because the mood outdoors is refreshingly light-hearted, entertaining a large group often seems more manageable and more like an opportunity for you to let go of the details and simply have fun.

life when dressed in layers of sheer linen; wooden lawn chairs get a fresh face when given a quick coat of paint and coloured cushions. Fill in any gaps in the space with items from the indoors that are strong enough to stand up to the elements. Enamelware and acrylic are durable choices for outdoor tableware. Canvas and twill are the finest in washable fabrics. Wicker patio pieces make an easy transition to a lawn for extra seating.

If you decide to entertain in the evening, choose lighting that both illuminates and enhances the mood. Fairy lights laced through

Outdoor entertaining is an invitation to be creative. Celebrate a special event in a festive setting and it will be remembered long after the candles have gone out.

As you plan your event, survey the space at hand and assess what furnishings and accessories you'll need and what pieces can be nimbly updated. Make the most of all things light and portable: director's chairs, folding tray tables, card tables, huge rugs and oversize cushions. A location close to the house, like a porch, courtyard or sunny back garden, affords the luxury of proper chairs borrowed from the dining room or upholstered pieces lifted from the living area. Accommodating large parties often requires creative thinking when it comes to furnishings, but the spirit of the outdoors encourages innovation. A weathered picnic table gains new

a row of hedges or a patio pergola lend a soft, starry luminescence, while lanterns hung from porch beams or tree branches cast a more concentrated glow. When placed in hurricanes or luminarias, twinkling candles add instant depth and drama to the festivities.

The sky is literally the limit when it comes to decorating an outdoor party. Accent a table with bunches of herbs, seashells, autumn leaves, acorn place-card holders or flowers fresh from the garden. If you're near the sea, fill bowls with sand to anchor pillar candles. Any embellishment that draws attention to the surroundings is sure to keep guests lingering long after dusk.

A Barnside Celebration

Entertaining large groups often requires a little ingenuity. When you're planning dinner for a crowd, a countryside location yields extra space and adds an element of surprise. Pair rented banquet tables draped in linen with hay-bale benches for a classic barn party with a modern twist.

Sometimes the first day of warm weather is all it takes to inspire inventive thoughts of an outdoor get-together. Celebrate the season and plan a celebration around the local colour and fresh appeal of the countryside. With the right mix of wildflowers, colourful linens and portable fixings, the exterior of a rustic barn can act as a backdrop for a memorable event with friends.

When you are entertaining, the style of the furniture is often less important than the details that dress it up. Standard folding tables set end-to-end provide ample space for a large gathering and their utilitarian surfaces can be easily hidden with several yards of chocolate-coloured raw linen. Bales of hay make a witty statement when lined up as benches on either side of the table. You can either leave them as they are or add a cushion at each place setting. They're the perfect size for seating a row of guests and fit right in to a country setting. Fragile dinnerware might not always be the best choice for outdoor dining. Instead, why not forgo plates completely in favor of colourful take-away containers or snap-lid lunch boxes? These clever alternatives can be filled, stacked and easily carried from kitchen to table.

Restaurant take-away containers, *left*, in black and white, add a city touch to a country setting. Serving dinner in stackable boxes cuts down on table-clearing time. **Red enamel camp lanterns**, *right*, find an original and convenient home on a rake brought out from the barn.

Design Details

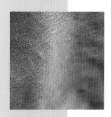

Colour Palette

Neutral colours, such as brown, white and black, are often called "naturals," and with good reason: they're soothing tones inspired by nature and the natural materials we see every day, such as wood, stone and earth. Use a palette of neutrals when you want to highlight a bright accent colour – the way brown linen emphasises splashes of red on the table here – or to frame an outdoor vista in rooms with a view. Muted earth tones and simple black and white make the best background for vibrant hues.

Materials

Myrtle An evergreen shrub that can grow up to 3.5 m (12 feet), myrtle is a wonderful hedge and wall plant that you can use to create a defined area outdoors. Its long, dark green leaves are lustrous and it has very fragrant white blooms when it flowers, usually in midsummer.

Raw linen A long-wearing fabric made from fibres from the woody stem of the flax plant, linen is twice as strong as cotton and lustrous due to the fibre's natural wax content. The threads of raw linen vary in thickness, resulting in an irregular surface.

Oleander Rose and bay oleanders are attractive evergreen shrubs that can grow up to 3 m (10 feet). They bloom from summer to mid-autumn and flowers vary in colour from creamy yellow to pink to red. Oleander is poisonous, so exercise caution in places with young children and pets.

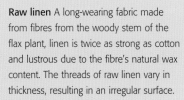

It's fun to dress up the rustic exterior of a barn with details that blend country sense with urban sophistication. Here, the table setting offers all the convenience of disposable goods, with twice the style. In lieu of paper, a washable linen-bolt tablecloth has a white stripe sewn directly down the centre for a ready-made runner. Red checked tea towels – used as napkins – and bright acrylic tumblers lend cheerful accents of colour. Add a brand-new wheelbarrow for an easy-to-transport ice chest and a vintage toolbox as a caddy for condiments or coffee and dessert. Complete the setting with country music.

Brand-new paintbrushes, *left*, are placed at each seat for guests to sweep away straw from clothing. **A wheelbarrow**, *above*, acting as an ice chest, holds bottles of cold beer and sparkling water.

A Polished Patio

The beauty of a patio lies in the way it blurs boundaries between inside and out. Treat yours as a natural outdoor extension of the living room, decorated with livable style and ready for anything from glamorous cocktails to an hour or two of quiet lounging.

On a gorgeous afternoon, a patio becomes an appealing alternative to the living room – a place to read a magazine, relax with family or enjoy cocktails with friends. The perfect patio is highly versatile, able to swiftly transition from a sunning and resting place to an idyllic spot for dining or entertaining. Choose furniture that enhances this flexibility and that can be easily configured to create different seating arrangements. An oversize armchair and ottoman can be pushed together to form a chaise or set up as a chair and coffee table for trays of drinks.

When furnishing a patio, choose woods that weather nicely and keep in mind the natural bleaching effect of the sun. Because teak is a tropical hardwood with a high oil content, it's one of the most resilient choices for outdoor furnishings. Over time, teak fades to a golden brown and eventually turns a silvery grey. Fabrics for upholstery and decorative accents should also be durable and fade-resistant. Washable, tightly woven materials, like twill or poly canvas, stand up to the elements and their softness serves as a reminder of a patio's leisurely sensibility.

The wide arm of a deck chair, *left*, is the perfect size for resting a freshly shaken martini, hors d'oeuvres and a hand of playing cards. **A dark wood cocktail tray**, *right*, offers a pleasing contrast to the blond wood furniture while keeping drinks, snacks and games close at hand.

This outdoor room is clearly defined by three exterior walls and the border of a lush lawn. A pergola overhead further encloses the space and supports an overhang of climbing plants. Adjustable pendant lamps can withstand heat and moisture more readily because they were designed for kitchen use. The clean-lined furnishings carry indoor comfort outside, but the selection of botanicals connect this space to its surroundings. Potted lemon trees, olive trees and large white planters filled with flax mirror the landscaping. Bougainvillea and climbing sweet pea frame the space and bring vibrant garden elements onto the patio.

A group of teak club chairs, *left*, creates an outdoor entertaining area that's easily adaptable to the patio's ever-changing activities. **Rows of botanicals**, *above*, from cut stems in shapely glass vessels to flax planted in tall white pots, serve as moveable "walls," granting added privacy as needed.

Design Details

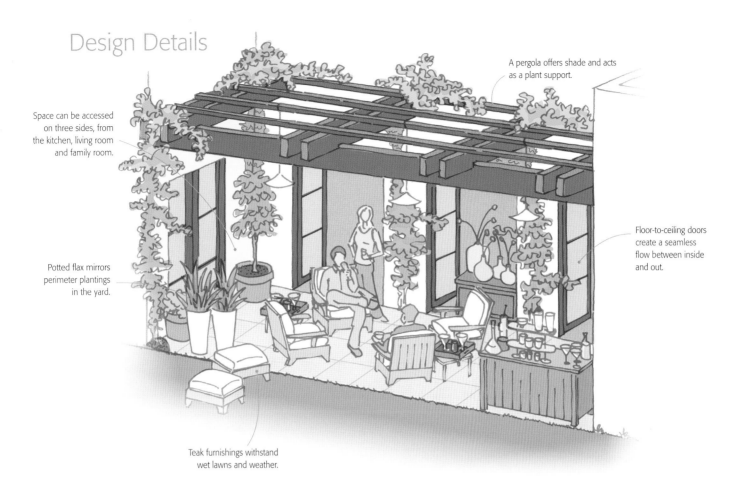

A pergola offers shade and acts as a plant support.

Space can be accessed on three sides, from the kitchen, living room and family room.

Floor-to-ceiling doors create a seamless flow between inside and out.

Potted flax mirrors perimeter plantings in the yard.

Teak furnishings withstand wet lawns and weather.

Colour Palette

Whether light and honey-toned or deep and earthy, brown has a nice way of offsetting bright colours from the warm side of the colour wheel. On this patio, the walnut of deep-stained trim and honey hues in sanded teak furnishings are foils for red bougainvillea and green climbing sweet pea vines. As unlikely as this trio may seem, the mix works because the neutral wood tones ground the high-key hues of the flowers.

Room Plan

Because they usually do without drapery, carpet and wallpaper, most outdoor rooms take their colour schemes from the surrounding plants and materials, which is something to keep in mind when choosing structural materials, flowers and shrubs. Pavers of sandstone, slate and pea gravel all lean toward the cool end of the colour wheel, while materials such as teak, sisal and wicker tend to be warm. Here, white stuccoed walls and a poured cement floor keep everything in balance, from the brilliant "draperies" of climbing vines to the fringe of a green lawn "rug".

Materials

Teak A ruddy blond tropical wood that weathers to silvery grey if left untreated, teak can also be sealed to keep its original colour.

Flax This annual plant with shiny, narrow leaves and blue flowers is a dramatic addition to outdoor spaces and requires little care as a container plant.

Twill This durable fabric is tightly woven and has a raised diagonal weave. Sun-treated twills stand up to outdoor use best.

A Midsummer Supper

There's something spectacular about dining outdoors. A casual collection of chairs and a little candlelight are all you need for an outdoor dinner party that's unique and comfortable.

Perhaps it's the mingling of candlelight and starlight that suggests endless creative possibilities when you're entertaining outdoors. The absence of structural boundaries allows the surrounding landscape to charge the atmosphere. A table set against the dramatic backdrop of a hilly vista or a nearby garden creates a pleasing contrast in scale for approaching guests. Furnishings in pale colours or white, like these mismatched chairs, are ideal for use outdoors in the evening because they appear to glow beneath lanterns or moonlight.

Everyday jars, *left*, are transformed into a canopy of lanterns with tealights. **Monogrammed napkins**, *above*, make a creative alternative to bread baskets. **A collection of dining chairs**, *right*, shows three different styles unified by colour.

How to Accent Outdoor Dining Tables

Hosting a meal in the outdoors, whether it's an intimate cocktail hour or a grand family feast, is the perfect chance to be creative with memorable details that enhance an open-air setting. Begin with lighting that sets a mood and theme for an event: paper lanterns have a playful look; pierced votive holders are another atmospheric option. For a centrepiece, display nosegay arrangements in jam jars next to tealights or choose potted miniature succulents, which guests can take away with them at meal's end. In lieu of standard place cards, look to clever substitutes like vintage postcards, Polaroid photos or objects found in nature.

A centrepiece of potted herbs, *opposite*, arranged in a galvanised drink caddy, makes a fragrant focal point on the table. Guests are encouraged not only to pick a fresh garnish for their drinks but also to take home a plant for their herb gardens. **Fresh lisianthus**, *left*, placed in small juice glasses, rest atop shapely glass candlesticks. In the evening, these informal vases can be move down to the table when candles take their place. **A tablecloth weight**, *above*, made from a tiny portrait frame tied with a ribbon, keeps linens in place and serves as a thoughtful tribute to the guests of honour.

relaxing

Sometimes just finding the time to catch up with friends or enjoy a quiet hour alone can seem an elusive pleasure. The fuller our lives become, the more difficult it is to resist being busy, from answering phones and just-landed emails to the stack of mail waiting on the kitchen worktop. Happily, a perfect day can bring us to our senses, luring us outdoors to enjoy what only sun, sky and a whispering breeze can restore: the sound of the earth and our own inner calm.

Making true relaxation a regular habit instead of a rare break begins with creating your own your own special place, enclose it in banks of lavender or an arbour of roses; plant a butterfly bush if you like a bit of company; install a bird feeder or a birdbath if you prefer an audible reminder that you're at home in nature.

Convenience is the key to relaxation, so look for storage ideas that keep your favourite amenities close at hand. Anticipate everything you might want for a restful afternoon. Set a cooler of cold drinks within reach of a sunbathing area. Keep extra sweaters in a cedar-lined trunk parked next to an outdoor fireplace. Create a portable bookshelf

Slowing down to the pace nature keeps is relaxation in its truest form. Take advantage of a hidden corner or an open stretch of grass to create a secluded space to escape.

private outdoor "world away". Whether it's on the patio just outside your bedroom window or in a shady spot hidden among distant trees, design a hideaway that will satisfy your need for comfort and your desire for a quiet read, an afternoon nap or an hour's meditation. If there's a place you can lay permanent claim to, think about investing in the daybed of your dreams and dress it to suit your personal notions of bliss. If your best option is a site that requires ferrying supplies across the lawn, think light and portable: a rope hammock to sling between branches, a rolled-up yoga mat with a travel pillow tucked inside, a mosquito-net canopy, a thermos of herbal tea. To mark it as

by filling a wagon with books and magazines you can wheel out to your favourite reading spot.

Style your nest to suit the time of day you most enjoy or are most likely to be able to slip away. If morning is your best time, maybe all you need to recharge for the day ahead is a comfy chair set out on the lawn and the morning paper. If you enjoy spending quiet time with a friend, add a second chair and a table for two. If watching the sun go down with your feet up is your ideal, make it a daily pleasure as well. Find yourself a rooftop or a shaded porch, pull up a chair and relax. Following nature's pace may be all that's needed to restore your own.

Relaxing by the Pool

Long summer afternoons are prime time for gathering around a pool for hours of sun and fun with family and friends. Make comfort your top priority and set up a casual poolside spread of tapas and refreshments, with resort-style lounge chairs nearby that invite guests to relax in style.

The weekend has finally arrived and so has the weather you've been waiting for since January. It's time to relax, take a swim in the pool, cool off in the shade and catch up with the family. Make your pool area the place where everyone wants to gather, with plenty to eat and drink, comfortable lounge chairs and a relaxed hospitality that lets you enjoy the day as much as your guests do.

For a simple and summery look, select sturdy outdoor furnishings with clean lines in easy-care materials. Keep maintenance to a minimum by choosing poolside lounge chairs in weatherproof woods like teak; they won't require annual refinishing and will eventually fade to a muted gold or grey. Pools naturally come with a hard surface area, so you'll want to offset a stone or concrete apron with generous and soft seating. Dress your lounge cushions with bright terry covers made from beach towels. They're easy to sew and are soft, quick to dry and can be thrown in the wash. Provide plenty of extra towels, tightly rolled, to be used as headrests or back supports. Offer guests a selection of flip-flops, magazines, paperback novels, fans and spray bottles filled with cold water; all are inexpensive amenities that will instantly inspire relaxation.

A wire glass carrier, *left*, keeps a collection of flip-flops in various sizes dry and close to the pool. **Oversize beach towels**, *right*, in summery hues, can be easily sewn to cover the cushions of poolside chaises.

Take a tip from the best seaside resorts and offer your sunbathing guests an equally inviting place to escape during the course of a long day by the pool. It can be a large permanent canopy extending from the house, a retractable awning or a freestanding white canvas pavilion. To make this shaded retreat feel more like a room, dress up the floor with a sisal rug and add an alternate lounging area with chairs and a table set with a brightly coloured spread.

A tray of drinks, an array of snacks and a place to lounge let you savour every poolside moment.

To best handle the weekend crowd, provide plenty of hooks for guests to hang their towels and shelves to stow their belongings. Place hats, sunscreen, games, toys, floats, water wings and other pool items nearby in baskets. Drape the table in appetising colours and follow with food and drinks to match: a jug of sangria, tapas, cheese, plus other snacks and refreshments for the kids.

Frozen lemon and lime wedges, *left*, work like ice cubes to keep drinks chilled and add a hint of citrus flavour. **Paper lanterns**, *right*, in graduated sizes, create a soft glow and a festive atmosphere when the sun begins to set.

Colour Palette

Use colour to refresh and enliven an outdoor relaxing space. The vibrant shades of orange and green used here are naturally reminiscent of such summer pleasures as ripe fruit and newly cut grass. Set against broad strokes of crisp white, these fresh colours reveal their cooler side (think abundant scoops of summer sorbet). Used in striped table linens, they call to mind classic tropical patterns and also reference the juicy flavours of the table's refreshments.

For those who read or rest in the shade or for friends in search of quiet time far from the pool splashers, a wooden daybed layered with colourful pillows is just the thing. Stools and benches are perfect for a space that plays double-duty for entertaining. They can be scattered around for extra seating, pushed together to make a coffee table or stacked to serve as a sideboard. Serving trays in co-ordinating colours can ferry tumblers of chilled soup and other easy-to-serve treats straight from the kitchen.

Throw pillow and towels, *left*, in a fresh, summery palette play off the colours of the vibrant plantings throughout the yard. **Lacquered or plastic trays**, *above*, are easy to clean and carry and they offer a bright accent of colour against natural wood furniture.

Materials

Acrylic Virtually unbreakable, acrylic is celebrated for its practicality outdoors, yet its translucence allows it to mimic the look of fine glassware. Available in a full spectrum of colours, acrylic tableware is an essential for outdoor entertaining.

Coreopsis The showy yellow, daisy-like flowers of coreopsis bloom in profusion all summer long. A good choice for poolsides and other exposed, sunny areas, coreopsis will literally grow like a weed (it's common name is tickweed). 'Badengold' and 'Goldfinch' are two attractive varieties.

Terry cloth Known for its softness and superior absorbency, terry cloth has a looped surface and is usually woven from cotton. Because it washes well, dries fast and is unharmed by humidity, it's also an ideal upholstery or pillow covering for furnishings in most outdoor settings.

A City Hideaway

An armful of cotton rugs, pillows and other rich accents is all it takes to turn a common-space garden or small city courtyard into a relaxed urban setting and a stylish tea party for two.

Outdoor escapes may be hard to come by for city dwellers, but a shared area, whether it's a rooftop or a courtyard, is prime living space for reinvention when a sunny day arrives. Bring in your own soft goods to create a lounging area that's as portable as it is inviting. Let a permanent table act as the central platform, then build around it with layers of rugs and pillows for plenty of low, casual seating. Everything here can be easily packed up and transported in baskets in a single trip, including a petite tea service and dessert dishes, which echo the Moroccan flavour of the setting.

Moroccan-style poufs, *left* and quilted pillows offer comfortable, portable seating for impromptu outdoor parties. **A bed of nasturtium,** *above,* requires little care to flourish and creates a vibrant edging. **Layers of rugs,** *right,* establish a simple colour theme for this urban retreat.

A Fireside Retreat

Anyone who has watched the flames of a campfire understands the appeal of an outdoor fireplace. A fire draws people together and fills a space with an inviting glow. In an outdoor living room designed for year-round relaxation, a built-in fireplace is a welcoming addition.

A wood-burning fireplace is the perfect focal point for an outdoor seating area, whether you live in a moderate climate that invites year-round outdoor living or simply want a place to enjoy the crisp air of an autumn weekend. If you have the luxury of building from the ground up, there are a few basic fireplace designs to choose from, ranging from a circular stone fire pit to a brick-chimneyed hearth. The style and materials you use will depend on space requirements and other practical needs. Will your fireplace be used as a barbeque, an outdoor oven or simply a spot for relaxation? If new construction isn't an option, consider a portable fire pit or a freestanding chiminea made of ceramic. Here, an exterior hearth was added to a stone chimney that also serves the living room's fireplace inside.

For a seating area that can be changed with ease between seasons, choose furnishings in natural colours and basic materials. Wood, zinc and seagrass all weather to a rich patina over time and require little maintenance if kept out of the rain. In hot summer months, cool colours freshen up the space, while earth-toned reds and cognac hues make it warm and inviting as autumn approaches.

Pillows in autumnal hues and rich materials, *left*, make an antique Balinese daybed more comfortable for relaxing in front of the fire. **All-weather sailcloth drapes**, *right*, are grommeted to easily slide closed and guard against sun and wind. They also soften the strong lines of the timber frame.

Outfit a fireside area with an abundance of cool-weather comforts. Pile sumptuous throws and pillows in handsome storage baskets. Cover the floor with a tightly woven rug, like this colourblocked wool kilim, that resists stains while adding warmth underfoot. Shelves stocked with little pleasures, such as reading material, mugs or marshmallows for roasting, make guests feel at home and keep this retreat in constant use throughout the year.

Extra seating pulled up to the fire, *left* and a cosy throw are essentials for warding off a chilly autumn breeze. Tucked under the coffee table, a basket of books serves as a portable library that's easily moved from room to room. **A glass canister**, *above*, keeps marshmallows fresh for roasting.

Design Details

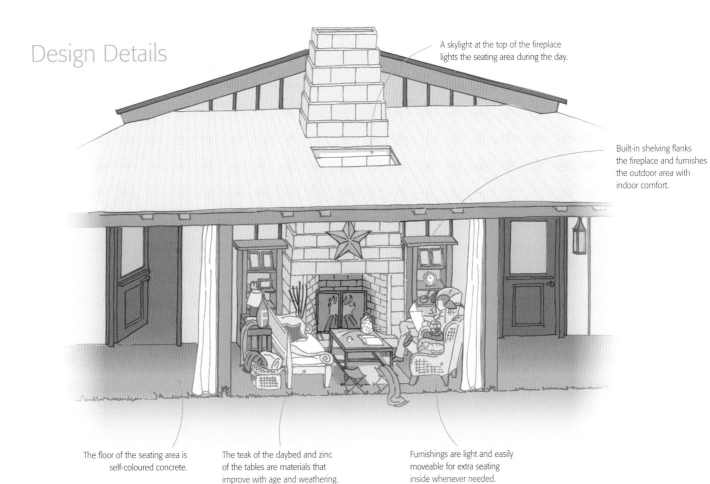

A skylight at the top of the fireplace lights the seating area during the day.

Built-in shelving flanks the fireplace and furnishes the outdoor area with indoor comfort.

The floor of the seating area is self-coloured concrete.

The teak of the daybed and zinc of the tables are materials that improve with age and weathering.

Furnishings are light and easily moveable for extra seating inside whenever needed.

Colour Palette

A space with a fireplace as its primary focus benefits from a colour palette with deep shades of burnished red and brown, which reflect the same level of warmth and depth as a crackling blaze. Blending these rich tones of red and brown with lighter strokes of pale gold and khaki in furnishings and fabrics ensures that the area feels intimate but also airy and cool enough for use during warmer months.

Room Plan

This outdoor seating area is part of a wraparound porch that shades the house on three sides. The front section is more than 12 m (40 feet) in length and its layout mirrors that of the open-plan interior: the space is informally divided to accommodate several activities at once. The comfortable seating area around the fireplace gives way to a more private reading nook around the corner to the right. The arrangement of wing chairs and daybed at the fireplace is comfortable for both large, convivial gatherings and smaller, more intimate groups.

Materials

Seagrass This aquatic grass has a durable fibre that's similar to straw. Resilient to humidity and moisture, seagrass furnishings will not warp in the outdoors.

Sailcloth Used to make sails and tents, sailcloth is a strong, heavy canvas fabric made of cotton, linen, jute, polyester or nylon.

Zinc Prized for the soft appearance of its finish, zinc is a strong, lightweight metal that weathers to a beautiful patina over time.

Comfortable Outdoor Seating

Who isn't seduced by the prospect of time spent outside in the sun with the Sunday paper or chatting with an old friend? Finding furnishings that can withstand the elements while still offering "indoor" softness can be a tricky prospect. Use the easygoing quality of the outdoors to inspire simple solutions. Colourful cushions nestled into a wooden bench or a steel-framed chair not only promise comfort but add style and colour. Every outdoor seating area should include a few lightweight, portable pieces for flexibility – tables that keep drinks and reading material close by and chairs that can be pulled right up to the warmth of a fire pit.

Under the cover of an overhang, *left*, this seating area is protected from sun and rain, making it easy to add little luxuries. **Smaller-scaled furnishings**, *top*, arranged in a circle, can accommodate up to seven people; a soft abundance of cushions and throws add volume to make the space appear larger. **A duet of garden chairs**, *above*, creates an intimate conversation area when positioned facing one another within a hedged, secret garden. **A patchwork quilt**, *right*, gives extra padding – and a touch of pattern – to a built-in bench for fireside seating on decking.

refreshing

What could be more revitalising than diving into a crystal blue lake on a hot summer day? One of the most satisfying rewards of spending time outdoors is indulging in all the refreshing possibilities that water presents: a tranquil soak in a hot tub, an invigorating swim in a pool, a cool rinse in an outdoor shower. If you live near the sea or have a pool, it's easy to enjoy the naturally restorative effects of water. If you don't, creating your own retreat – whether a simple shower or an outdoor spa – needn't be a faraway dream.

customised stage for an outdoor shower using mismatched tiles, arranged decoratively under a professionally plumbed outdoor showerhead.

If the night is warm and the sky is clear, nothing is more luxurious than a long bath beneath the stars. If you don't have the desire or the space for a fully fitted hot tub, create a screened spot for soaking by setting potted plants around a tub in a corner of the garden. Antique enamel tubs stand up well to the elements and, if plumbing is a challenge, are easy to fill with a hose and a few buckets of hot water.

Few things inspire the imagination and awaken the senses quite like water. Whether it's a pool or a hot tub, a space for bathing outdoors refreshes the body and mind.

The thrill of bathing in the open air recalls the freedom and relaxed atmosphere of childhood and the convenience of having a place to wash up on the way back from the beach or after a day in the pool cannot be matched. Outdoor showers require little in the way of space and upkeep and they can be easy to install. With a basic readymade model, an outdoor shower can be put to use quickly with a simple attachment to a nearby hose or spigot. Look for styles with a treated wood base that's slatted for drainage and durable enough to weather changes of season. Then seek out a secluded spot (a spectacular view is a plus) in which to set it up. You might even create a

Whether your dream is an open-air bath or a built-in lap pool, outfitting an outdoor area with all the comforts of a spa can make it an idyllic retreat. Look for accessories and storage pieces that are well equipped to handle the effects of water. Attach a stainless steel shower caddy to a tree branch near your shower for soaps and loofahs. Outside you can plan a space dedicated to relaxation and repose and ignore many of the practical aspects required indoors. Have fun and create surprises. Stock towels in easy-to-carry picnic baskets, use a water-ski rope instead of a towel drying rod, set up a daybed near an outdoor tub and keep special little luxuries on hand.

Creating a Private Oasis

The perfect spot for a secluded bathing hideaway might be as close as your own garden. Take inspiration from the setting nature provides, whether it's a cluster of trees or a towering formation of boulders. Find a private corner for a bathing area that blends luxury with rustic simplicity.

Who hasn't dreamed of having a quiet corner in which to bathe in solitude under the open sky? Nothing is quite as relaxing as taking a long soak, then wrapping up in a plush robe and lounging with a good book. Except, perhaps, doing so in a luxurious retreat built within a small circle of trees or a natural rock enclosure. Bring the dream to life by starting with the floor. Whether it's a ready-made platform or specially commissioned decking, a base of weather-treated wood is important because it will not only have to support a bathtub but must drain water, too. From there, all you need is a freestanding bath, which can be hooked up to a warm-water hose fitted by a plumber or filled by hand.

Adopt a practical decorating approach to help make this spot a calming retreat. Choose furnishings with streamlined designs and removable cushions that can be whisked away when dark clouds appear. An outdoor lounge chair fitted with a stone-coloured cushion blends in with the natural environment. At certain points in the day, extra shade may be necessary. Draping a swath of sheer fabric over a sturdy branch or on a rope strung between trees filters the sun and offers added privacy to further define this secluded area.

A sheer white canopy, *left*, provides a touch of drama and shade when it's needed. **A wire-mesh basket**, *right*, is lightweight for carrying rolled-up towels and bathing luxuries; it's also perfectly proportioned for a small space.

Design Details

Colour Palette

Uncomplicated hues of stone grey, cool white and the pale taupe of weathered wood come together for a natural trio to wrap around a serene outdoor bathing space. In this setting, with its surrounding boulders and trees, the colour palette has already been decided by nature. But think about employing a neutral palette like this one in any bathing space, indoors or out. Neutrals are sophisticated, versatile and make a calming visual backdrop for any retreat environment.

It's the sensory details that make a spa experience feel rejuvenating – a palette of calming scents and quiet colours and textures that are soft and inviting. Plant fragrant herbs close to the tub so that rosemary, lavender and mint for a scented bath are right at your fingertips. Use a sheepskin rug as a bath mat; it feels wonderful underfoot when you're stepping out of the bath and it's easy to roll up and bring inside. Have a plank of wood cut to size for use as a bath tray, and keep rechargeable lanterns close at hand for a little atmosphere to accompany a sunset soak.

Materials

Organdy This sheer fabric is commonly used for making curtains and canopies. Inexpensive and finely woven organdy has a tight weave that's effective as mosquito netting for screening out insects. Easy to launder, organdy lends a romantic air to outdoor rooms of all kinds.

Douglas fir A highly durable softwood, this native North American evergreen tree is now widely planted in Britain and is an excellent choice for decking and flooring. New or reclaimed pine has a rich colour and will withstand years of exposure to the elements.

Rosemary A highly aromatic herb from the mint family, rosemary is traditionally used in aromatherapy as a rejuvenating stimulant. Its oils may be added to the bath to stimulate circulation and ease muscle pain.

A porcelain bathtub, *left*, gets a new life outdoors, painted pale grey to blend with its rocky surroundings. **Rechargeable lights**, *above* or portable battery-powered lamps, offer safe lighting after sunset. After charging on a base unit, they'll glow through the evening.

A Spa Sanctuary

ROOM TOUR

Pools have always been a favourite place to enjoy the company of friends and refresh the mind and body. Poolside, the calming effects of water set a relaxed pace. Surround your pool with beds of lushly scented plantings, then add a large sofa to sink into after a swim and enjoy the summer.

Summer is a time of year to savour. Warm weather tempts us outdoors and encourages lazy afternoons relaxing with friends and family. Climbing temperatures also make the pool area one of the great rooms of summer – a place to escape the heat and refresh body, mind and spirit. Make your poolside the perfect summer destination by giving it the restorative atmosphere of a spa, complete with space for quiet reflection and casual entertaining.

When furnishing the pool area, choose designs that offer comfort while highlighting the site's main assets. In place of or in addition to, the usual bank of lounge chairs, create a seamless dissolve between indoors and out by fitting a comfortable sofa with rugged casters and wheeling it out to the water's edge. Outdoors, a sofa becomes an element of surprise and a supremely comfortable perch for enjoying an afternoon with friends. Loose covers in twill (a durable, washable version of denim and one of the best outdoor fabrics available), and the sofa will remain easy-care all summer long. A smooth concrete pool apron allows you to move furnishings to follow the sun or shade and a poolhouse offers convenient cover in case of rain.

A durable stainless steel juicer, *left*, positioned over a corner of the pool, keeps fresh juice just a few strokes away. **A sleek trio of plastic stools**, *right*, doubles as extra seating or easily reconfigured side tables. Their lightweight design and weatherproof material make them a practical poolside choice.

Colour Palette

White, grey and blue are all sky colours, so what better choice for a pool whose surface reflects the heavens in every type of weather. Blue and white is always a tranquil colour combination that reminds us of water. But for outdoor rooms in general and spa areas in particular, grey is another smart colour choice. On the practical side, it won't show dirt and the colour becomes softer and prettier as it fades. On the decorative side, calming grey is just right for encouraging contemplative relaxation.

Materials

Yarrow Tall and graceful, with a spicy scent similar to sage, yarrow is easy to grow. It thrives in heat and poor soil conditions, loves full sun and attracts butterflies. Use yarrow to create a carpet of blossoms by a pool or plant euphorbia for a similar effect.

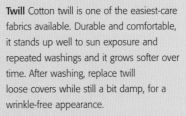

Twill Cotton twill is one of the easiest-care fabrics available. Durable and comfortable, it stands up well to sun exposure and repeated washings and it grows softer over time. After washing, replace twill loose covers while still a bit damp, for a wrinkle-free appearance.

Lavender This perennial herb blooms summer to autumn, is fragrant and can withstand heat and drought. Plants will grow up to 60 cm (2 feet) high and can be sown or used in containers to hide pump machinery near a pool. As an added benefit, lavender attracts butterflies.

Beds of fragrant herbs and rows of aromatic plantings frame this clean-lined pool in nature's most soothing tones. Hardy perennial herbs, like lavender, mint, rosemary and sage, do well in most climates; their therapeutic fragrances add a welcome note of calm to the spa-like atmosphere. A moveable canvas umbrella provides shade where needed and extra-large bath towels can be spread on the ground, draped on the sofa or used as cosy throws on chilly evenings.

A loose-covered sofa, *left*, deserves a second look when rolled up to the water's edge. A weatherproof teak mat makes an ideal accent and feels good to bare feet. **Lightweight straw baskets**, *above*, provide convenient storage for towels and double as garden holdalls for gathering herbs from poolside plantings.

A Camp Shower

Finish off a day of sand and surf with a rinse in a one-of-a-kind outdoor shower. Setup is easy; all you need is a household garden hose plus a few clever details to make the space your own.

Before heading into the house, a quick rinse with the hose is must for sandy feet. Make washing faster and more fun by jumping into your own garden shower. A simple outdoor shower can be set up in minutes by attaching it to a standard garden hose and setting it alongside a nearby tree. Waterside living is playful and relaxed, so suspend a hula hoop to hang a shower curtain for privacy (favourite fabrics are always welcome). Position wooden stools close by for must-have shower items, like a mirror and shaving tools and be sure to keep one stool cleared off for waiting your turn.

A shower curtain, *opposite*, hung from a hula hoop, offers privacy and a pair of stools serves as an outdoor "vanity". A simple towel bar, *left*, is easily fashioned from a length of rope. Woven fisherman's nets, *above*, allow soap to air-dry.

A hanging wine rack, *left*, can remain on a covered porch and weather the summer nicely. It makes a clever, space-saving dispenser for fresh towels, magazines and bottles of spring water. Keep the pool area tidy by hanging a canvas holdall from the bottom rung and stowing sunblock, swim gear, sunglasses and other small essentials.

A narrow built-in cabinet, *above*, keeps rolled-up towels and baskets of sunscreen organised and easy to locate. Fold striped towels in alternating directions for a stylish and tidy display.

How to Equip an Outdoor Bath

If you're provisioning a hot tub, pool or outdoor bathing space, supply it with everything needed for self-service pampering. First, you'll want plenty of towels: white is easiest to clean and simple to accessorise with from season to season. If you prefer a little colour, blue fades nicely in the sun (think of your favorite pair of jeans); if you want a lot of colour, outside is just the place to indulge your desire for bold stripes and patterns that might be too much for a small indoor bathroom. Tuck lotions, potions and flip-flops into woven plastic holdalls, which make stylish, waterproof storage baskets that stand up to wind and weather.

A hot tub with a view, *left*, is a place you'll want to linger without making lots of trips back to the house. Hot tub how-to calls for having a plentiful supply of towels, drinking water and sunblock at the ready. **A beveled mirror**, *top*, outfitted with hooks is hung on an exterior wall alongside an outdoor shower. **Woven plastic holdalls**, *above*, make ideal storage solutions for outdoor bathing spaces. They're lightweight and impervious to the elements. Hang a few on hooks and colour-code them to identify their contents.

inspiring

For some, the sun is the only place to be when warm weather arrives. For others, a private, shady spot in which to read, dream or garden approaches perfection. Reconnecting with the natural world fortifies the creative mind. An hour spent among the plants, by the water or simply enjoying your own garden space is naturally inspiring. Outdoor areas for entertaining and dining are a warm-weather institution, but you can also assemble an outdoor studio for your creative pursuits – a place where supplies can be kept and inspiration can visit.

beach mats, flat-weave rugs and blankets can be unfurled just about anywhere to create an instant outdoor "room". Add a market umbrella or sheer fabric screen to create privacy and temporary seclusion that is easy to dismantle and carry away (along with the mat) for another day.

An art studio can be set beneath the spreading branches of a tree with just a portable easel, a folding chair and a picnic basket supplied with brushes, paint and paper. Create a garden retreat from a collection of potted plants on a balcony, rooftop or windowsill.

Create a space where creativity rules: equip an outdoor studio, whether portable or permanent, with everything at the ready for the weekend gardener or artist within.

You won't need very much to begin, just a favourite pastime or a long-neglected hobby. Focus on all the ways the exterior world ignites your creativity. Perhaps you love to plant flowers or relax in the countryside or write by the water's edge. Next, decide whether your studio must be portable or if it can be permanent. For most of us, the challenges of space and location dictate portability. Luckily, whether you dream of the water but are landlocked or live in the city but crave the country, the possibilities abound.

A little green space in a park and a featherlight seagrass mat may be all the equipment needed to roll out a studio at a moment's notice. In fact,

For the perfect writer's retreat, bring a sturdy folding table out onto the lawn for an afternoon. Keep a laptop computer, journals, pens and other writing essentials ready to travel in a lap desk, tackle box or train case – all of which will keep supplies organised and protected, too. Small suitcases are excellent storage options for holding camera equipment, binoculars, manuals or notebooks for recording bird sightings from your perch on a porch swing. Whatever your passion, every landscape offers a bounty of options. The trick is to find – or to create – a simple, spirited venue and then dedicate a little time to immersing yourself in a favourite practice.

A Rooftop Garden

You don't need acres of lush rolling lawns or even a garden to reap the rewards of a cutting garden. A dozen or so pots filled to the brim with quick-growing plants and softly scented flowers changes even the tiniest urban terrace into a secluded garden getaway.

For some city dwellers, an occasional walk in the park offers plenty of respite from urban life. For others, nothing but the real thing, up close, will do: hands in potting soil, a daily check on the unfurling of each new bud, eight different shades of green crowding the balcony, the windowsill and the rooftop. If gardening is your favourite way to recharge your creativity, don't let a small space cramp your style.

When planted in sleek, lightweight pots mounted on casters, container plants – whether herbs, flowers or vegetables – can easily be moved around to take advantage of the day's changing light or to update the look of a garden. Placed around the perimeter of a terrace, potted plants create an attractive border that provides a screen for privacy while leaving your view unobstructed. When selecting varieties for a container garden, bear in mind the amount of sunlight your outdoor space receives each day. Roses, sunflowers and geraniums need at least six hours of direct sunlight every day; hydrangeas, impatiens and hostas do well in the shade. Perennial flowers, like dianthus and rudbeckia, are well suited to a terrace environment because of their easy maintenance and robust growth. Aim for a graceful flow of plant materials, interspersing low, full-foliage varieties with taller plants.

A miniature topiary tree, *left*, is embellished by a circle of glass reflecting balls. **A seagrass chair and ottoman**, *right*, do well in an outdoor environment and their small scale complements a compact space.

When choosing lighting for an outdoor space, try solar-powered options to help conserve energy and cut down on maintenance. Most turn on automatically in the evening and maintain their glow for up to ten hours before needing sunlight for recharging. Different lights require different hours of sun exposure to work, so take this into account when selecting a style. Freestanding lamps can be set on tables and stake-mounted styles can be pressed down into flowerpots, allowing rearrangement as needed.

A wall of windows, *left*, frames a terrace garden against a dramatic urban landscape. Softly glowing solar-powered orbs arranged on a metal table add a sculptural note to the lighting scheme. **Solar-powered lanterns**, *above*, must be positioned where they can get a minimum of six hours of sunlight.

Design Details

Colour Palette

Flowers and foliage provide all the colour needed in an outdoor garden room, whether on the lawn or on the rooftop. Choose ruby coreopsis, pink foxglove and bright russet and yellow rudbeckia. Add lavender and white accents with scabiosa, marguerite daisies and erigeron. Leafy greens are an undisputed favourite for creating a fresh interior atmosphere and they're just as pleasant when you make them a planned part of a container garden using ornamental leaves and grasses.

Materials

Laminated wood A composite of woods bonded with a thin outer layer of veneer, laminated wood was pioneered in furniture design by Finnish designer Alvar Aalto in the 1930s. Moisture-resistant and easy to wipe clean, laminated wood adapts well to sheltered outdoor settings.

Rudbeckia A favourite perennial for container gardens, rudbeckia is known for its golden yellow flowers with russet and dark brown centres. Cutting back blossoms encourages repeat flowering and protection from extreme heat will help it thrive.

Scented geranium The scallop-shaped leaves of these flowers release intriguing and beautiful scents. Orange, lemon, rose and chocolate-scented varieties are all available, in colours ranging from white to red. Scented geraniums grow well in pots, hanging baskets and borders.

When furnishing a compact outdoor space, choose pieces in keeping with the smaller scale in order to preserve a sense of openness. Versatile pieces, like an ottoman, can be put to use as a planting stool, side table or extra seating. Here, a compact potting bench holds everything an urban gardener requires and its tools and containers are chosen for their good looks as well as their functionality. When the sun goes down, it's easily cleaned up and pressed into service as an outdoor bar for entertaining.

Laminated wood chairs, *left* and a powder-coated steel table come clean with just a quick wipe of a damp cloth. **A compact potting bench**, *above*, offers an organised station for planting, repotting and arranging flowers from the cutting garden.

An Inspiring View

A hanging daybed presents a brand-new view of the water. Outfitted with soft pillows and waterproof storage, it transforms a covered porch into a favourite destination.

Taking a little time to reflect on a waterfront or lakeshore view is a classic lazy-day pleasure. Make the most of the experience by forgoing standard seating in lieu of a more inviting daybed that's sturdy and generously outfitted. Paint a simple twin bed frame in all-weather marine paint and use industrial-strength chains to suspend it from the rafters of a porch or covered dock. Add sunproof cushion covers that wash easily to give the seat all-weather appeal. A rust-resistant metal trunk makes a smart accent and stores all that's needed for a relaxing afternoon.

Twin hanging lanterns, *above,* offer light for reading or relaxing. **A telescope and an audio player,** *right,* invite stargazing and birdwatching to music. **Deep-blue marine paint,** *opposite,* helps make this hanging daybed water-resistant.

How to Find Creative Inspiration

In these busy times, who couldn't do with a little less interruption and a little more inspiration? Tradition has it that gardens, pools of water, smooth spheres and winding spirals help focus the mind and encourage insight, though it may seem a tall order for such small things. Since all of these elements are as beautiful as they are meditative, why not use them to make your outdoor space a truly tranquil sanctuary? Fill a planter with water hyacinths and lilies to create a floating garden. Place gazing spheres along a pathway or a circle of stones near a favourite perch, to soothe your senses and inspire your creativity.

A planter of succulents, *above*, provides a low-maintenance garden that will stand up to the most difficult growing conditions: harsh sun and heat by a pool or wind on a rooftop garden or city balcony. **Stone circles**, *right* and labyrinths reflect spirals found in nature (think of the inside of a nautilus shell) and are ancient patterns found in many cultures throughout the world. Tracing the path of a circle or labyrinth is said to calm the spirit and stir the imagination.

A water feature, *above*, is always present in traditional Japanese gardens. The fluidity of water represents timelessness and is thought to unify the garden with the sky through its reflection.

A stone basin, *above left*, transforms a trickle of running water into a soothing fountain. Eastern tradition also suggests that the sound of running water connects our thoughts to the present moment and places us in harmony with earth.

Glass globes filled with water, *left* and gazing balls of all kinds, provide a calming point of focus that helps the viewer let go of everyday distractions and concentrate on the task at hand.

getaways

The fast pace of life today can make a spontaneous getaway seem out of reach. But even if a weekend away is out of the question, try planning a retreat close to home. Whether you crave solitude or the company of a friend, pack up as much as you can carry and head for the nearest corner of the back garden, terrace, roof garden or local park to create an outdoor room for an afternoon or the whole day.

City living may not offer the luxury of a large private lawn, but don't underestimate the promise of a balcony or a shared courtyard. With container plants. Hang lanterns or strings of lights from a nearby tree branch for a twinkling canopy to enjoy long into the night.

If finding a patch of greenery requires a trip away from home, pack up your car, your bicycle or your backpack with lightweight and compact amenities. Choose practical furnishings suited to the scale and mood of your particular retreat: folding lounge chairs and a camp stool are perfect for an afternoon of sunning in the park; a portable awning and a picnic lunch can be easily packed into your car boot for a get together; a

Some of the best getaways don't require a weekend out of town. A local park or your own balcony can be just the right place to have an outdoor adventure.

a little imagination, any of these can be transformed to pull off the effect of a genuine escape. You're not in your living room, you're not in your kitchen. You're officially off-duty and that's what counts.

Close to the house, the simplest way to carve a getaway space from any outdoor annex is to define it with natural plantings. Edge a balcony with pots of hardy perennial herbs, like lavender, rosemary or sage. Shut out a discordant view and muffle the sounds of the world with a fast-climbing honeysuckle or clematis. Enclose yourself in a section of the courtyard behind neatly clipped laurel or sweetly scented jasmine

pair of baskets over the back of a bicycle is all it takes to transport a blanket and a few magazines to a hilltop hideaway.

Use weatherproof baskets or canvas holdalls to carry all the necessities of a one-day holiday: neckroll cushions, swimsuits and sunscreen and a thermos full of lemonade by day; candles, a radio and a takeaway dinner by night. Choosing the right storage, whether it's portable or permanent, makes it easier when it's time to go, too: everything can be quickly stowed and carried home again. No plane to catch or suitcase to pack. Just you, a few favourite amenities and some good weather to keep you company.

A Seaside Escape

It only takes a few hours to set up a summer retreat for reading, sunning and relaxing with Sunday morning coffee. In almost any natural setting, a canvas tent and a few comfortable furnishings can convert a small plot of land into a quiet hideaway with its own private view.

Escaping your daily routine doesn't mean you need to abandon the comforts of home. We all crave occasional solitude, but finding the time to take a holiday can be a challenge. Creating a warm-weather getaway – one that can be set up almost anywhere for the season – is easier than you might expect. Just look to the practicality and versatility of a classic canvas tent. Stake your claim a short distance from the house, whether on a sunny spot in the garden or a grassy corner overlooking water, be it a river, stream or pond.

No longer just an affordable place to unroll a sleeping bag, a tent becomes its own fully furnished corner of the world when equipped with a wood-burning stove, a camp lantern and the comforts of an indoor bedroom. When clouds gather, it also zips up quickly to keep the rain at bay. Make your getaway irresistible by including one or two substantial pieces that take it from an overnight campsite to a place where you could relax for days. A collapsible camp bed is infinitely more inviting than a sleeping bag. A refined club chair can be draped in a thick blanket and transformed into a place for outdoor daydreaming.

A wire lawn chair draped with a quilt, *left*, is lightweight enough to carry away and is just the spot for morning coffee and a view of the sunrise. **A one-room canvas tent**, *right*, is all you need to build a perfect escape.

Enjoying nature up close reconnects us with our surroundings and gives us a renewed perspective on the colours, textures and forms offered by the natural world. Such insight is our best barometer when designing an outdoor room that brings joy and satisfaction whenever it's used. Adaptable furnishings in timeworn materials – weathered paint, vintage metal, sun-bleached canvas – are the best choices for a getaway retreat.

The beauty of a tent lies in both its spatial limits and limitless possibilities.

Tap into this setting's down-to-earth spirit with a little innovation and a few outdoor camping tricks. Substitute rows of bungee cords in spots where shelving and racks would be used. When stretched between support poles, they provide ready storage for towels, newspapers and magazines. A hanging canvas cabinet keeps clothing out of sight and can be quickly folded up into a duffel bag when doing laundry.

Bungee cords, *left*, stretch between rope tent supports to make a handy drying place for towels or swimsuits. **A collapsible metal table**, *right*, is small enough to slip beside a camp bed but large enough to hold a jar of snacks, the newspaper and a travel alarm clock.

Colour Palette

A blue-and-white colour scheme with accents of red is the essence of summer itself. Muted ticking-stripe fabric is an old-fashioned classic that looks great on the lawn or by the water's edge, especially when you're decorating with a lot of plain cotton and twill. When exposed to full sun, the fabric fades to a soft slate-and-white colour combination. Berry red is a natural accent for this palette and makes the tent comfortable and handsome.

Materials

Canvas A heavy-duty fabric commonly used in the manufacture of sporting goods, tents and outdoor furnishings, canvas can be woven from linen, hemp or cotton. Water- and weather-resistant, canvas perfectly suits the casual, relaxed feel of an outdoor setting.

Grass Remember that the grass under your tent will yellow as it is denied sunlight. If you are able to, relocate your tent every so often to encourage new and healthy growth. And don't forget to appreciate the feel of the grass between your toes!

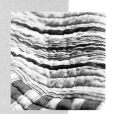

Quilt Made of two layers of fabric with a soft batting layer between them, quilts are stitched in patterns through all layers to prevent the filling from shifting. Use folded and rolled quilts in place of loose covers or cushions to soften outdoor furniture.

Defy the notion that tent-dwelling means "roughing it" by surrounding yourself with simple things that bring honest pleasure, such as an easy-to-use stovetop espresso maker that lets you hang on to a morning ritual and a mini battery-powered radio for music and news of the outside world. But don't invite in too many of these reminders; play up the real benefits of a tent by siting it where the sounds of crashing waves or flying geese make your getaway truly transporting.

A standard camp lantern, *left*, delivers extra light after the sun goes down. Snuggle under a quilt as you tuck into a cosy club chair to watch the tide roll in and out. **A battery-powered radio**, *above*, can add to the natural soundtrack of a seaside retreat.

How to Create a Workday Getaway

Who says office work has to be done indoors? Make the most of a sunny day and take your responsibilities outside. All you need for a portable, open-air office is a few square feet of unoccupied territory: a shaded lakeside hill, a small side terrace or a back patio will do just fine. Add a comfortable chair, a cold drink, a flat surface on which to balance a spreadsheet and a holdall or rattan basket to hold files and other workday essentials. While you're at it, pack up a cart and transform it into ready-to-travel storage for outdoor office amenities. With a little ingenuity, you can turn almost any location into a remote office that's a pleasure to use.

A little grey cart, *above*, is kitted out as a complete home office on wheels. A vintage LP case is perfectly sized to hold flat files, a well-padded laptop computer and a crate of standard office supplies (including a clock).

Adirondack chairs, *right*, set up by a lake, turn conference calls into a guilty pleasure. While you're waiting for that call, paddle a few laps in a canoe or set up fishing poles.

A portable workstation, *opposite*, makes it fun to work from home. The lounge chair, tray table and picnic basket all fold up so you can relocate to wherever the wind blows or sun shines.

Room Resources

At Pottery Barn, we believe that casual style is something you can weave through every space in your home, from front rooms to private havens. For this book, we scoured hundreds of locations to find perfect settings to create outdoor spaces just for you. We experimented with furnishings and accessories to find the best combinations for each space. The results? This collection of outdoor style ideas, which we hope will inspire and delight you.

Each location chosen for this book was unique and interesting. Here is a little bit more about each of the homes we visited, the style ideas we created and the individual elements that make each design tick.

A Family Garden Party

Rows of fruitless mulberry trees frame this dinner-party setting, which is adjacent to a vineyard, a tennis court and the estate's 1871 stone Victorian home.

Space Sited on 11 secluded acres, this estate features formal lawns and flower beds and a virtual arboretum of mature trees including oak, Douglas fir, maple and peach. Fragrant borders of star jasmine enclose a tennis court and serve as a divider to the vineyard.

Furnishings Farmhouse occasional tables, wicker chairs (painted black), Classic hotel table linens, Great White dinnerware, Classic red wineglasses, Tivoli cutlery, ash-wood chalkboard, galvanised party buckets, pillows made from Emily floral and Classic plaid bedding, all from Pottery Barn. Taylor green acrylic tumblers from Pottery Barn Kids. Hats from Hat Box, Mill Valley, CA.

Lighting Globe lights, giant hurricanes, pillar candles, all from Pottery Barn.

pages 14–21

Relaxed Lakeside Living

This boathouse and dock were built by the homeowner on a man-made lake that's used both for recreation at this country home and for irrigation of its vineyard.

Space Built as a shaded gathering place for a family who loves to waterski, the boathouse overlooks a windbreak of willow trees across the lake. The decking is a water-resistant composite of reclaimed wood and plastic.

Furnishings Westport corner sofa with ticking stripe slipcover, ottoman, café chairs, solid outdoor pillow, Roma barware, modern frames, all from Pottery Barn. Pegboard shelving from Hold Everything. Canvas holdalls from Lands' End. Laxne folding metal tables from Ikea. Awning-stripe pillow from Kate Spade.

Lighting Elliot sconces from Pottery Barn.

pages 28–33

Casual Beach Cookout

Located at the southern end of Lake Tahoe, this private sandy beach is part of a holiday rental that offers three lakefront acres and an historic alpine-style lodge.

Space The house was built in 1934. The living room features a huge stone fireplace and floor-to-ceiling lead-paned windows, which overlook the lake and the sandy private beach below. Accessed by a set of stairs that starts at a deck off the living room, the beach has dramatic views of the snow-capped Sierra Nevadas. An outcropping of granite boulders shelters the beach from wind.

Furnishings Westport corner sofa cushions, Cabana stripe pillows, Arctic cutlery, Great White dinnerware, galvanised three-tier stand, Classic hotel table linens, oversize shell bowl, all from Pottery Barn. Suncatcher chair from PBteen. Striped pillows from Ikea. Other linens from Williams-Sonoma. Roll-up tables from Cost Plus World Market.

Lighting Hampton lanterns with pillar candles and stakes from Pottery Barn.

pages 42–47

A Garden Barbeque

A family-friendly pool, patio and back lawn were just recently added to the shaded hillside property behind this country home. The house dates back to the late 1930s.

Space This newly designed back garden has both hardscaping and landscaping that's easy to maintain and durable. A flagstone patio requires little upkeep and plantings of petunias and ground cover need only regular watering. The apron around the pool is made of standard pavers that dry quickly and keep feet cool on hot days.

Furnishings Chesapeake extending dining table, benches, daybed and chaises; solid outdoor pillows; market umbrellas; café glassware; Classic cutlery; enamel party buckets and colanders, all from Pottery Barn. Polka-dot dinner napkins from Martha Stewart.

pages 54–59

A Tropical Courtyard

Custom-designed by the architect/homeowner, this Mediterranean-style villa features a main house, a studio building and a guest house around a walled central courtyard.

Space This T-shaped courtyard acts as a corridor from the front entrance to the main house, with a small fountain and towering shade trees along the way. The landscaping – designed by the homeowner's brother – focuses on sun-loving tropical plants, such as banana, bougainvillea and bird-of-paradise, as well as low-maintenance potted varieties of succulents, including jade and aloe.

Furnishings Megan chairs, Great White coupe dinnerware, heavy sham goblets, Tivoli cutlery, wine bucket, all from Pottery Barn. Table linens and tea towels from Tag. Woven chargers from Cost Plus World Market. Grosgrain belts from J. Crew. Acrylic tumblers and votive candle holders from Target.

Lighting Coloured glass lanterns and lantern stakes from Pottery Barn.

pages 60–65

A Napping Porch

The front porch is original to this late 1930s ranch. Located in a rural hilltop setting, the house was built by a family who operated the surrounding vineyards.

Space Classically designed as an outdoor annex to the house's front door, this porch extends the entire width of the structure. Steps run up the centre of the porch. Built of shiplap-style cladding with long floorboards painted with durable deck paint, this porch is built to last and designed to protect those who use it from both sun and rain.

Furnishings Seagrass sectional seating, glass display box frame, solid outdoor pillows, chunky basket-weave pillows, sisal runner, all from Pottery Barn. Side table from Ikea. Striped pillows sewn from vintage fabrics.

Lighting Enamel pendant lamp from Pottery Barn. Clip-on articulated lamp from Ikea.

pages 74–79

Daybed in the Shade

Modelled after a classic Southern-USA-style Colonial, this house features formal rose gardens, boxwood hedges, a wraparound porch and this arbor-covered sleeping space.

Space With an overhead pergola that's heavy with wisteria blooms in early summer, this shaded side porch offers fragrant access to a garden walkway. French doors lead to the dining area, and steps bordered by boxwood lead down to a swimming pool and circular arbor seating area.

Furnishings Megan slipcovered daybed, pickstitch quilt and sham, rustic stripe quilt, Classic bedding, Chloe matelassé bolster, Morrow chairs, Hampton bath cabinet, Classic grand phone, all from Pottery Barn. Blue blanket from Banana Republic. Dog figurines from Yankee Girl Antiques, San Anselmo, CA.

Display Cloud paintings from Oly, Oakland, CA.

pages 80–83

A Barnside Celebration

Located adjacent to a house that is said to have been built by General M.G. Vallejo, this traditional barn has stables that the current owners use to store garden supplies.

Space Adopting classic barn vernacular, this structure features painted white detailing over a chocolate brown color. Surrounding the barn are white oleander trees and rows of tall hedges that hide the barn from the rest of the property.

Furnishings Classic cutlery, red acrylic tumblers, retro radio, Bosphorous vases, all from Pottery Barn. Custom tablecloth sewn by Sima Kavoosi. Tea towels from Target. Wheelbarrow from Orchard Supply Hardware. Vintage horsehair paintbrushes circa 1930s.

Lighting Hampton enamel lanterns from Pottery Barn.

pages 90–93

A Polished Patio

As a transitional space between the house and the grassy garden, this patio was designed to visually connect the two spaces and offer a seamless flow from indoors to out.

Space Accessed on three sides by French doors leading into the living room, kitchen and family room, this 8 x 4 m (25 x 12 foot) patio can be viewed from almost anywhere in the house. The pergola-like structure overhead is made of redwood and helps support climbing bougainvilleas and sweet peas. Pots planted with lemon trees dot the patio and draw attention to the plantings of flax and mature olive trees throughout the yard.

Furnishings Chesapeake console, chunky basket-weave pillows, Bradford tray, Swank bar tools, heavy sham barware, all from Pottery Barn. Saranac teak furniture from Smith & Hawken. Tall white planters from Ikea. Vintage barware from The Other Shop, San Francisco.

Lighting Porter enamel pendant lamps from Pottery Barn.

pages 94–99

Relaxing by the Pool

This wine-country estate was renovated in the 1970s by famed designer Val Arnold, who added a pool house and planted sycamore trees for a French country look.

Space Originally designed solely for entertaining, this house was built with no pool and no bedrooms. Subsequent owners added a bedroom, a pool house and a pool and completely overhauled the landscaping. Apple and olive trees now dot the property and mingle with beds of lavender and decorative pools.

Furnishings Chesapeake single chaises, beach towels, market umbrellas, solid outdoor pillows, Chesapeake folding chairs and daybed, sisal rugs, Cambria tray, tapas serving set, acrylic tableware, all from Pottery Barn. Striped throw pillows from Les Toiles du Soleil. Tablecloth from Bed Bath & Beyond.

Lighting Small paper lanterns from Pottery Barn.

pages 108–13

A Fireside Retreat

This mountaintop retreat was built for a large extended family to enjoy year-round. The outdoor living room's design was inspired by a hacienda in San Miguel, Mexico.

Space The outdoor fireplace was custom built at the center of the house to serve as a welcoming beacon in the dark to approaching family and guests. A skylight at the top of the fireplace allows the sun to light the covered porch during the day. The columns that support the overhang are salvaged redwood and the roof is made of tin, a material purposely chosen to enhance the sound of rainfall

Furnishings Antique Balinese daybed, with Chesapeake daybed mattress from Pottery Barn. Seagrass wing chairs, patchwork rug, Gayle coffee table, sailcloth grommet drapes, pedestal vase, all from Pottery Barn. Zinc console from Swallowtail, San Francisco. Satin pillows from Target. Red vinyl pillows and woven plastic pillows from Linens 'n Things. Leather saddle stools from Barking Frog, San Francisco. Painted ceramic vase from Home, San Francisco.

Lighting Hammered metal lamp and tripod lamp, both from Pottery Barn. Wooden lanterns from Illuminations.

pages 116–21

Creating a Private Oasis

This outdoor bath is located on a three-acre lakefront getaway. The property includes a six-bedroom house built in 1934, a sandy beach and a grove of pine trees.

Space A small Douglas fir deck located just off the back door of the main lodge-style house is made into a private space by a circle of 13-m (42-foot) pine trees and several large granite boulders. Raised about 90 cm (3 feet) off the ground, this compact platform is fitted between boulders and trees and can be accessed by two sets of steps.

Furnishings Chesapeake chaise, Studio mirror, Classic terry towels, all from Pottery Barn. Wire baskets and organdy window panels from West Elm. Sheepskin rug from Ikea. Bath products from Hydra. Rechargeable candles from Candela.

pages 128–31

A Spa Sanctuary

Sited on hundreds of privately owned acres, this large family compound features a pool area designed to complement the surrounding mountain landscape.

Space The pool was built in the shape of a trapezoid – it's 17 m (55 feet) long and ranges in width from 3 m (10 feet) to 4 m (13 feet) at the far end – to create the illusion that it's extending into the backdrop. Plantings of lavender, wild grasses and yarrow were brought to the edge of the pool to refer to the surrounding landscape and seamlessly reflect the environment.

Furnishings Square sofa, rectangular market umbrella, waffle-weave towels, stainless steel juicer, all from Pottery Barn. Acrylic goblets from Williams-Sonoma. Prince AHA stools from Kartell. Grey towels from Target. Silver bowl from Ikea. White leather tray from Coach.

pages 132–35

A Rooftop Garden

With a view of the San Francisco skyline and the Bay Bridge from the cedar balcony, this modern, minimalist three-story home sits on top of a hill.

Space This 8 x 2 m (25 x 6 foot) north-facing balcony gets just the right amount of midday sun for growing both annuals and perennials in pots. Tall plantings screen the balcony from adjacent residences and can also be viewed through a wall of windows from the open-plan living area.

Furnishings Morrow chairs, seagrass chair and ottoman, all from Pottery Barn. Metal table from Emu through Design Within Reach. Rolling planters from Ikea. Potting bench from Smith & Hawken.

Lighting Solar stake lights from Gardener's Supply Company. Glowing solar globes from Frontgate.

pages 144–49

A Seaside Escape

The seascape is the focal point of this cliffside property overlooking the Pacific Ocean. The house was built of grey stucco to highlight the surrounding natural beauty.

Space Two low buildings are enclosed within grey stucco walls on top of gravel hardscaping that was designed to harmonise with the foggy vista. Closer to the cliff, cushioned Golden Gate grass and a Monterey cypress frame the view.

Furnishings Leather club chair, rustic stripe quilt and shams, patchwork quilt, Belmont stripe quilt, solid outdoor pillow, enamel tray, Tivoli Pal portable radio, all from Pottery Barn. Canvas tent, canvas hanging cabinet and stove courtesy of Grundman's Canvas. Folding bed frame from The Company Store. Mattress from McRoskey Mattress Co., San Francisco. Garden chair from Marin Resource Recovery. Vintage milking stool from France.

Lighting Vintage camp lantern.

pages 158–63

Glossary

Acrylic A clear thermoplastic polymer that is virtually unbreakable, acrylic is celebrated for its practicality in the outdoors, yet its translucent quality allows it to beautifully mimic the look of glass. Available in a spectrum of colours, acrylic dinnerware is a summer essential for outdoor entertaining.

Adirondack chair During the late nineteenth century, the Adirondack Park holiday spot in northeast New York became the inspiration for this style of outdoor furniture handcrafted with rough hemlock planks.

Bamboo Seasoned bamboo reeds form a very hard wood typically used to build houses in tropical climates as well as to construct fences and furniture. Bamboo laminate flooring – made of bamboo pieces that are steamed, flattened, glued together, finished and cut – is becoming an increasingly popular option for outdoor and indoor flooring.

Banana plant From the Musacea family of plants, the banana plant is actually a perennial herb rather than a tree. It grows best in warm, tropical climates, and its leaves can be damaged by strong winds, making it ideally suited for an interior courtyard.

Bougainvillea Also known as "paper flower," this woody flowering vine grows best in warm climates and full sun. With varieties in a range of red, pink orange, yellow and white, bougainvillea can also be potted indoors in colder climates and brought outdoors in the summertime.

Boxwood This bushy evergreen shrub, with its masses of dark green, oval leaves, is excellent for creating enclosure and division in an outdoor space. The traditional shrub used for mazes in formal gardens, boxwood takes well to topiary and is handsome when used as a pathway edging.

Canvas A heavy-duty fabric commonly used in the manufacture of sporting goods, tents and outdoor furnishings, canvas can be woven from linen, hemp or cotton. Use canvas inside and out for upholstery, pillows or drapes to bring a casual, relaxed look to a design scheme.

Cedar Reddish in colour, this aromatic softwood is resistant to decay. Often used for building outdoor furnishings, cedar ages to an attractive silvery grey patina over time.

Concrete Cement, sand, water and gravel form this strong, easy-to-maintain material. Most commonly used as a foundation material, concrete is cool to the touch, making it ideal for patios and outdoor rooms. Concrete can be integrally tinted in a range of hues that will maintain their depth of colour through years of wear.

Coreopsis The showy yellow, daisy-like flowers of coreopsis bloom in profusion all summer long. A good choice for poolsides and other exposed, sunny areas, coreopsis will literally grow like a weed (its common name is tickweed).

Cotton A lightweight fabric woven from spun fibres from the boll of the cotton plant, cotton is breathable and washable, which makes it the perfect all-season fabric. Long-staple or Egyptian cottons are the softest options for bedding, while sun-treated canvas and twills are better choices for outdoor furnishings.

Deck stain This stain- and moisture-resistant stain may be oil- or water-based and is flat. It is designed to withstand heavy foot traffic and prolonged exposure to water.

Decking Decking in Britain is mainly sourced from Scandinavia. Be sure that the company you use is a member of the Timbertrade Federation, who are commited to reducing environmental impact by sourcing their timber as sustainable timber, through the Foresting Stewardship Council (FSC).

Denim This heavy, twill-woven cotton fabric became popular in the United States during the California Gold Rush, in the form of work pants (jeans). Denim is a great washable loose cover option for outdoor spaces, becoming softer with every washing.

Douglas fir Timber from this Native North American evergreen tree is very durable. It is now widely planted in Britain and is excellent for decking and flooring. New or reclaimed Douglas fir has a beautiful colour and will withstand years of exposure to the elements.

Enamel A strong, scratch-resistant material created by fusing a glassy outer layer to metal, pottery or glass, enamel is often used to line ovens, cooking pots and cast-iron baths. It's also rustproof and has a long-lasting durability, making it ideal for dinnerware that's used outdoors or in humid climates. Dishware coated in layers of enamel has a distinctly retro look reminiscent of 1950s diners.

Enamelled metal Iron or steel is coated with a thin veneer of enamel to repel moisture and discourage corrosion.

Euphorbia Early-summer blooming euphorbia, along with lavender or yarrow, is a wise choice for naturalising a pool area. Euphorbia thrives in full or partial sun and does well in poor soil. The foliage stays green in climates with mild winters and its sulphur-yellow blossoms are attractive when the plant is grouped.

Flagstone An ideal material for garden patios, because of both its beauty and durability, flagstone is a hard, evenly stratified stone that cleaves into flat pieces that are well suited to paving.

Flax A tall, slender annual plant with shiny, narrow lance-shaped leaves and blue flowers, flax is a versatile addition to outdoor spaces. It requires little care and makes a dramatic container plant that can be used as a screen.

Impatiens While impatiens in tropical climates can flower all year, plants in other climate zones flower from early summer until the first frost. Equally successful in direct sunlight and shade, impatiens can be planted around the perimeter of a patio or used in smaller pots on tabletops.

Iroko Timber from Ghana that is very popular for use in garden furniture and fixtures. Similar to oak, but yellow in appearance that turns gold with treatment.

Jasmine Indigenous to tropical and subtropical regions, jasmine generally grows as a climber on other plants or on structures.

Laminated wood A composite construction of wood bonded with a thin outer layer of veneer, laminated wood is moisture-resistant and easy to clean.

Lavender This old-fashioned perennial herb blooms from summer to autumn, is highly fragrant and can withstand both heat and drought conditions. Plants can grow up to 60 cm (two feet) tall and can be sown in gardens or used in containers to screen pump machinery near a pool. As an added benefit, lavender attracts butterflies.

Limestone Composed of the mineral calcite, limestone comes from the beds of evaporated seas and lakes. Because it is softer than many stones, limestone weathers beautifully with age.

Lisianthus This summer-blooming annual produces white, pink, lavender, or purple flowers shaped like upturned bells. A hardy plant, it tolerates a wide range of growing conditions.

Mosquito netting This sheer fabric serves the practical purpose of keeping insects at bay, but it also makes an exotic decorative statement. Netting made of polyester or polyamide is very lightweight, long-lasting and more resilient than cotton netting.

Mulberry tree Rapid growth is a hallmark of mulberry trees. With their thick head of branches, fruitless male trees are ideal for shading. They are also good choices for growing near paved areas, such as around a patio, because they do not bear the staining fruit that falls from the female trees.

Myrtle An evergreen shrub that can grow up to 4 m (12 feet), myrtle is a wonderful hedge and border plant that you can use to create a defined area outdoors. Its long, dark green leaves are lustrous and it has highly fragrant white blooms when it flowers, usually in midsummer.

Oleander Rose and bay oleanders are attractive evergreen shrubs that can grow up to 3 m (ten feet). They bloom from summer to mid-autumn and flowers vary in colour from creamy yellow to pink to red. Oleander is poisonous, so exercise caution in places with young children and pets.

Organdy This stiff, sheer fabric is commonly used for making curtains and canopies. Inexpensive and attractive organdy has a tight weave that's effective as mosquito netting for screening out insects. Easy to launder organdy lends a romantic air to outdoor rooms.

Pea shingle Typically used in aquariums, pea shingle is a mix of small, smooth stones. The stones come in many muted colours and can be used effectively in an outdoor space in various ways, such as anchoring tabletop pillar candles in hurricane lamps or paving walkways.

Pegboard Board perforated with regularly spaced holes into which pegs or hooks can be fitted, this inspired invention came along in the 1950s. Pegboard can turn any wall into extra storage space and offers a flexible grid to accommodate outdoor gear of different shapes and sizes.

Petunia Hardy and easy to grow, petunias flower all summer long. A single plant will produce hundreds of blooms and its full foliage and mounding growth make it a natural as a container plant. Use petunias to create a low privacy screen around the perimeter of a porch.

Porcelain This type of hard pottery is fired in the kiln at extremely high temperatures, giving it a strong, resilient nature. Porcelain is typically used in hardworking indoor spaces, such as bathrooms. Because of the material's resilience, porcelain tiles are also a good choice for outdoor patios.

Raked gravel Typically used in Japanese Zen gardens, raked gravel can infuse an outdoor space with an air of serenity. A bed of raked gravel beside a pool or outdoor pond can be combed to mimic the rippling of water.

Raw linen A long-wearing fabric made from fibres obtained from the woody stem of the flax plant, linen is twice as strong as cotton and lustrous due to the fibre's natural wax content. The threads of raw linen vary in thickness, resulting in an irregular fabric surface.

Rosemary A highly aromatic herb from the mint family, rosemary has long been used in aromatherapy as a rejuvenating stimulant. Planted around a patio or potted as a centrepiece on a tabletop, its fragrance makes an appetising addition to an outdoor dining space.

Rudbeckia A favourite perennial for containers, borders and cutting gardens, rudbeckia is known for its delightful golden yellow flowers with russet and dark brown centres. Cutting blossoms will encourage repeat flowering and, while the plant likes full sun, protecting it from too much heat will help it thrive.

Rush matting Woven from any of a variety of tufted marsh plants with cylindrical, hollow stems, rush matting has been used as a floor covering since the Middle Ages. Because rush matting is strong, resilient and textural, it makes a functional and visually interesting outdoor flooring alternative.

Sailcloth Typically used to make sails and tents, sailcloth is a strong, heavy, plain-weave canvas fabric made of cotton, linen, polyester, jute or nylon. Sailcloth can be used for upholstery fabric or cushions.

Scented geranium The scallop-shaped leaves of these flowers release intriguing and beautiful scents. Orange, lemon, rose and chocolate-scented varieties are all available in colours ranging from white to pink and lilac to red. Scented geraniums grow well in containers, hanging baskets and borders and thrive in full sunlight.

Seagrass A commercially grown aquatic grass, seagrass produces a durable fibre that is similar to straw and smoother than coir or jute. Resilient even when exposed to high humidity and moisture, seagrass furnishings will not warp or crack, making them superior to wood in such situations.

Sisal A flexible fibre made from the leaves of the agave plant, sisal is softer to the touch than its lookalike, coir. It is commonly woven into textural, durable flat rugs that hide dirt and hold up well in high-traffic areas, such as entrances.

Succulents Succulent plants are perfect for potting because they require relatively little soil to survive, which allows you to pot several different types in the same container. From the same family as cacti, succulents have thick, fleshy stems and leaves that make them extremely drought-resistant and hardy.

Teak Indigenous to the warm, humid climate of Southeast Asia, teak wood is an ideal choice for outdoor furnishings. In fact, its rich lustre improves with age and weathering, so teak adds a polished, permanent look to other furnishings in outdoor spaces. The high oil content of teak makes it watertight and resistant to warping and insect damage.

Terra-cotta A hard, semi-fired, waterproof ceramic clay, terra-cotta has been used in pottery and building construction for centuries. Terra-cotta tiles are typically used for patios and roofs, while terra-cotta planters and pots hold everything from herbs to small trees.

Terry cloth The classic toweling fabric, terry cloth has a looped surface, usually made of cotton, that is naturally absorbent. Because it washes well, dries fast and is unharmed by humidity, terry is an ideal upholstery or pillow covering for furnishings in most outdoor settings.

Timber treatments Tanalised timber is treated timber that is usually beneath decking. Decking timber should always be treated regularly with a suitable external treatment, whether varnish or oil, depending on use. There are various preservatives, oils and sealer available. There is a non-slip sealers for use on high wear areas and steps. Treat decking regularly to preserve good looks and the life span of the wood.

Twill This durable fabric is tightly woven, usually of cotton and has a raised diagonal weave. Sun-treated twills stand up best to outdoor use.

Weatherproof fabric The dense weave of canvas, sailcloth and other fabrics can be treated with Teflon (a fluorocarbon) to repel water and resist sun damage. Some outdoor fabrics are made of treated and coloured acrylic fibres; the colour is added when the material is liquid, so it can't fade or wear away.

Wicker A mainstay in outdoor rooms due to its sturdiness, wicker is crafted from bamboo or rattan canes. Usually woven on a wooden frame, it can weather exposure to the elements. Lloyd Loom is the most famous example.

Wisteria The perfect leafy canopy for a sleeping porch, wisteria screens sunlight by day and lets the stars peek through at night. This woody-stemmed climber blooms in early summer and thrives in full sun. Near an entrance, it provides a fragrant welcome.

Wrought iron A very pure form of commercial iron, wrought iron has a low carbon content, which makes it resistant to rust, an ideal attribute for furniture left outdoors year-round.

Yarrow Tall and graceful, with a spicy scent similar to sage, yarrow is easy to grow. It thrives in heat and poor soil conditions, loves full sun and, like lavender, attracts butterflies. Planted in drifts or clumps, it creates a colourful carpet of blossoms by a pool.

Zinc Prized for the soft appearance of its finish, zinc is a strong, lightweight metal that weathers to a beautiful patina over time. Used to create galvanised metal (zinc-coated iron or steel), zinc resists corrosion, making it a good choice for outdoor furnishings.

Index

Acknowledgements

Project Editor
Martha Fay

Copy Editors
Peter Cieply
Elizabeth Dougherty
Laurie Wertz

Designers
Adrienne Aquino
Madhavi Jagdish

Illustrators
Paul Jamtgaard
Nate Padavick

Indexer
Ken DellaPenta

Photography Assistants
AJ Dickson
John Robbins

Stylist Assistants
Julie Maldonado
Barbara Myers
Amber Tomasello

Lead Merchandise Coordinator
Mario Serafin

Merchandise Coordinators
Nick Castro
Darrell Coughlan
Scheffer Ely
Terri Fredlund
Paul Muldrow
Frank Simeone
Simon Snellgrove

Weldon Owen thanks the photography and editorial teams for their creativity and stamina in producing this book and acknowledges the following people and organizations for their invaluable contribution in:

Allowing us to photograph their wonderful homes
Laura Alber, Kurt Ashurst, John & Gretchen Berggruen, Nilus & Jennifer De Matran, Scott & Julie Drummond, Larry & Gina Everson, Charlie & Alexis Glavin, Robert & Kelli Glazier, Peter Haywood & Maggie Salenger Haywood, Laurie & Victor Ivry, John Paye and Jackie Goode at Fairwinds, Ivy Rosequist and John Staub

Supplying artworks or props
David Agrell, Kurt Ashurst, The Gardener, Mike and Linda Grundman at Grundman's Canvas, Nancy Coltes at Home, Janus et Cie, Sima Kavoosi, Modern I, John Paye, Mario Serafin, Timeless Treasures and Atlas Imports (San Jose, CA) for the poufs, throws and tea service on pages 114–15

Catering on location
Kass Kapsiak and Lorraine Olsen (Catering by Kass)

Providing assistance, advice or support
Jim Baldwin, Leonie Barrera, Lee Bottorff, Garrett Burdick, Chris Capporino, Rebecca Forée, Arin Hailey, Meghan Hildebrand, Linden Hynes, Anjana Kacker, Dawn Kurnava-Dickson, Francine Lasala, Jessica Morrison, Matt Roech, Celine Spencer and Colin Wheatland, as well as Owen Bingham, Victor Ruiz, Charles Williams, Chris Wilson and the rest of the staff at Pottery Barn (Corte Madera, CA)

Author Acknowledgments
I would like to extend my gratitude to Virginia Bell, Sally Davies, Karol Jackowski, Leigh Flayton, Eden Grimaldi, Zoe Ryan and Corey & Bryan Barberich for all their support and encouragement. I would also like to offer my heartfelt thanks to Shawna Mullen and to Sarah Lynch for her fine eye and exceptional editorial insight.

Photographer Acknowledgments
I would like to thank Emma Boys, for an amazing ability to keep an entire creative team simultaneously happy; Michael Walters, for brilliant styling and never-ending passion—you inspire many; Mario Serafin and his merchandising crew—you people really hold the shoot together; and my wife, Eszter, a constant support, whether near or far from me.

All photography by David Matheson and styling by Michael Walters, except for:
Page 47 (top Material), page 79 (middle Material), page 99 (bottom Material), page 121 (middle Material), 138 (right), 153 (top and right), photography by Dan Clark. Page 122 (left), photography by Alan Williams. Page 139 (two on right), photography by Hotze Eisma and styling by Anthony Albertus.